Tastefully written, **Red Hot LoveNotes for Lovers** is specific, practical, often poetic and rich with creative ideas and inspirational insights. **Dr. John Gray, Ph.D.,** Author
Men Are From Mars, Women Are From Venus &
Mars and Venus in the Bedroom

Laced with provocative ways to communicate and stimulating ideas that excite, **Red Hot LoveNotes for Lovers** belongs on your nightstand! Read before bedtime and get ready for Grrreat Sex!
Laura Corn, Author
101 Nights of Grrreat Sex

Larry James has done it again! He's focused on yet another aspect of loving relationships with wit and wisdom. This time he explores sexuality with rare sensitivity and great creativity.
Gregory J.P. Godek, Author
1001 Ways to Be Romantic

Larry James speaks from the heart. His words carefully craft a message of hope that inspires couples to work together in a spirit of love and understanding. **Red Hot LoveNotes for Lovers** can be a profoundly healing experience; first of self, of the relationship and of one's own sexuality. The powerful effect of his work in the area of relationships can change your life.
Jack Canfield, Professional Speaker, Co-author
Chicken Soup for the Soul series

Red Hot LoveNotes for Lovers reaffirms basic beliefs that shape the sexual side of relationships and inspires the application of effective sexual communication. Larry James offers his insight in an understandable way with passion and compassion. You must read it!
Mark Victor Hansen, Professional Speaker, Co-author
Chicken Soup for the Soul series

Red Hot LoveNotes for Lovers is another carefully written, challenging and beautiful "must read" book from Larry James. Lovers will find inspiration blended with encouragement that loving sex is worth working at and many suggestions about how to do it!
Dr. Larry Losoncy, Ph.D.
/Family Therapist

Larry James speaks f̶ ⋯ ⋯ ⋯ have all
encountered at one ti⋯ ⋯ **Red Hot**
LoveNotes for Lovers ⋯ ⋯ he joys of
passionate monogamy. ⋯ ⋯ smile.
⋯ , President
Persona⋯ ⋯ roductions

Also by Larry James

BOOKS:

How to Really Love the One You're With
Affirmative Guidelines for a Healthy Love Relationship

LoveNotes for Lovers
Words That Make Music for Two Hearts Dancing

The First Book of LifeSkills
10 Ways to Maximize Your Personal and Professional Potential

AUDIO CASSETTES:

A Relationship Enrichment LoveShop™
An interactive workshop designed to help you fit the pieces of the relationship puzzle together in a healthy way!

Red Hot LoveNotes for Lovers

The Importance of
Great Sexual Communication . . .
and Other Essentials
for Extraordinary Hot Sex

Larry James

Red Hot LoveNotes for Lovers

The Importance of Great Sexual Communication . . .
and Other Essentials for Extraordinary Hot Sex!

A Career Assurance Book ~ First Edition

Copyright © MCMXCVIII ~ Larry James

RedHot LoveNotes. . . ™ and LoveShop™ are registered
trademarks of Larry James

Printed in the United States of America
Library of Congress Catalog Card Number: 97-69727
ISBN 1-881558-04-5

Distribution in the United States and Canada by
LPC Group, Chicago ~ 800-626-4330

Cover design by Lightbourne Images ~ 800-697-9833
Interior design by Graffolio ~ 608-784-8064

Published by:
Career Assurance Press, P.O. Box 12695
Scottsdale, Arizona 85267-2695 ~ 800-725-9223

Publisher of Books Designed to Enhance Your Personal and Business Relationships

Contents

Acknowledgements

A special "thank you" to Patty Kellogg, M.A., for her last minute proofing notes. Patty is a former journalist and college teacher. She is currently a counselor in private practice in Vancouver, Washington.

I humbly acknowledge the Source from which all knowledge flows.

Dedication

To my best friend, partner and forever lover,
Sandy Charveze . . . my wife.

Her love, understanding, acceptance
and willingness to be vulnerable
is the inspiration for my work.

She is loved . . . unconditionally!

Introduction

This book is dedicated to love partners* who are deeply committed to the idea of passionate monogamy, fidelity and having lots of fun together in the bedroom! Sex is fun and pleasure is good for you! For a committed relationship to be worthy of great sex it must have the honor and sanctity of marriage.

Men and women who view themselves as great lovers already are always looking for a better way to increase their mutual pleasure. The intention of this book is to encourage those in committed relationships to become connoisseurs of the art of creative sexual expression, openly and fully, with words *and* deeds.

It is my hope that this book will stimulate your imagination in a way that opens up sexually stimulating conversation between couples who already know each other intimately; this book is for lovers who trust each other enough to openly express their love for each other in erotic ways and love partners who are willing to devote the time to prolonged expressions of love.

The tips and suggestions in this book will help you invent new fantasies to prepare you and your partner for gourmet sex. They are ideas you can use to build to that magic moment when you unselfishly give orgasm to your lover. Making love is a natural expression of the Divine nature of love. It needs variety. It deserves it. It requires paying special attention to discover new and exciting ways to sexually arouse your love partner.

Most of my life I have been reasonably uninhibited when it came to talking about sex, what I liked, what I did not like. When presenting my "Relationship Enrichment LoveShop," the subject of sex often comes up. Someone once asked how MY sex life was. "Incredible," I answered. Sandy, my wife, was sitting nearby. She nodded with an approving smile. Because I was hearing so many horror stories from couples who were experiencing trouble in the bedroom, I began talking more openly about sex in an inquiring way and what I heard made me realize that there was a need for simple guidelines for great sex for couples.

In addition, since I began hosting the Mars and Venus Chat Room on America Online, I have answered thousands of relationship questions for Dr. John Gray, Ph.D., author of *Men Are From Mars, Women Are From Venus*, sent by e-mail. This helped me stay focused on the many aspects of relationships, sexual and otherwise. In studying the problems presented by e-mail from both women and men, I have discovered workable solutions that assist couples in committed relationships to experience the closeness they desire and so richly deserve.

I have learned that great sexual communication is imperative! It is one of the keys to a healthy, sexual relationship . . . *and* it is the third key. The first key is to have a great relationship with yourself. The second key is to fully share that relationship with someone you love – having 100% of the time you are with them be about keeping the lines of communications open for the benefit of the overall relationship. The extraordinary hot sex I have with Sandy, my wife, is great because we are BOTH committed to utilizing the wisdom of the three keys to a healthy sexual relationship.

Relationship problems always show up in the bedroom! When they do, and to move past them, it is important to be in open and honest communication with your love partner . . . all the time. When the relationship is humming along and both love partners are focusing all their energy on having a great relationship, great sex is the reward.

Almost every sexual problem has an underlying communication problem. To make love you must get close enough *for* love. Resentment, anger and issues left hanging can keep the wedge driven deeply. You cannot be irresistibly approachable with unresolved issues and all the emotions that go with them.

Talking about them – in loving ways – brings them out into the open. The tension begins to ease. What you can't talk about owns you! Talking gets them out of your head and on the table where you can deal with them. It is impossible to solve problems that no one is willing to acknowledge or talk about.

This book makes the assumption that you are both doing "whatever it takes," working *together* to make your relationship better than it already is and that you want more meaningful conversation, intimacy, and great sex! Relationships are something we must work on all the time, not only when they are broken and need to be fixed.

It is my belief that an active and healthy sex life, based on mutual consent and respect between love partners, is an important component of physical and mental well-being. Sex is a private matter and each person has a different opinion of what sexual practices or levels of discourse are appropriate.

The inability to discuss your sexual needs can cause your relationship to potentially be an unhappy marriage. I believe the divorce rate could be significantly lowered if couples who lie next to one another each night, wanting to connect, needing to connect, but afraid to communicate their wants and needs with words or touch, could agree to have better communication – specifically more "loving" conversations. Working on yourself comes first, working on the overall relationship always comes second and working on your sexual relationship comes in a close third. Two people who share their lives must be able to share what is on their minds so they can share their bodies for the enjoyment of mutual pleasure.

Here is a tip that will help you get more from this book. While YOU are reading it, mark the passages that are important to you with a colored highlighter. Then give the book to your love partner requesting that he or she do the same, marking important passages with a different colored highlighter. Take some time to carefully review the passages your partner has marked; make note of what is important to him or her. You need to know what is essential for your partner's happiness. Next, openly and honestly discuss what you have read – TOGETHER!

Caution: Resist the urge to mark the passages you KNOW your love partner NEEDS to read. When the student is ready, the teacher appears! Let the teacher be the book. . . not you. Let your love partner read and get from the book what he or she needs to learn. It rarely helps to push your own stuff on someone else. It often only causes resentment or drives a person further away.

By the way, any reluctance (or refusal) by your love partner to FULLY participate in WORKING TOGETHER on your relationship, regardless of the way you BOTH choose to do that (counseling, attending relationship & personal development seminars TOGETHER, implementing this idea of reading and discussing the book TOGETHER, etc.), is a RED FLAG!!! Therapy is always a wise choice.

This book will help you learn how to make love with the same person for the rest of your life . . . never letting age be your cage and without having sex become boring. It will help you create trailblazing intimacy.

The magic comes in awakening the intention within to trust yourself enough to pass through the doorway of responsibility into new sexual arenas. Enjoy!

Celebrate Love!

Larry James
Scottsdale, Arizona

---

*Do not be misled by the term "love partner." Your love partner is that person with whom you are in a committed, monogamous love relationship.

Red Hot LoveNotes for Lovers

**The Importance of
Great Sexual Communication . . .
and Other Essentials
for Extraordinary Hot Sex**

Larry James

Red Hot LoveNote. . . And in the end,
the love you take is equal to the love you make.
— The Beatles

Red Hot LoveNote. . . The first rule of making love is to present a body that is tastefully clean! Become a clean sex machine. Take personal hygiene seriously. There is no greater turn-off than offensive body odors from partners who have yet to learn to offer their bodies as if on a silver platter, ready to be devoured sexually by their partner. An unclean body can spoil the mood very quickly. Shower or bathe in scented water. Use a fragrant shampoo. To make sure unpleasant odors do not return, use an unscented deodorant. Dab a splash of your favorite cologne or perfume on or near the parts of your anatomy that might be visited by your lover. If you smoke, don't smoke before making love or better yet, quit. Kissing some-one who has just had a cigarette is like licking the bot-tom of an ashtray. Yuck! Stay clear of garlic or onions before connecting with your lover. Brush your teeth. Use mouthwash. Make your whole body suitable for the sexual feast.

Red Hot LoveNote. . . Would you like to know how to fast-forward your sexual experience with your partner from boring to bliss? Someone once said, "If sex is great in a relationship, it's only 10% important. If it isn't, it's 90% important." In other words, if your sex life is in the pits, it's the relationship you must pay attention to, not sex! Great sex does not guarantee a great relationship. When you can work together on the relationship as a team, the relationship will get better. Great sex is the reward.

Red Hot LoveNote. . . *For Women Only* ~ "You, fake orgasm??" Women who fake it rarely ever make it to a higher level of sexual awareness or experience. Some women can and do reach orgasm and some women won't, can't or don't. It's your body and you get to do with it whatever you choose. If you say you are reaching orgasm and don't, he will never really learn how to give you the pleasure you so richly deserve. This is a lie! Be his teacher. Tell the truth! Let him know that sometimes you will and sometimes you won't and it's not about HIM. It's your choice! Just because you did not reach orgasm does not mean you failed to enjoy the experience. Tell him so. If he is doing something right and you are almost there, let him know. He cannot read your mind and, believe it or not, most men cannot tell unless you have a body-shaking, earth-moving orgasm!

Red Hot LoveNote. . . In order to have extraordinary hot sex, you must communicate sexually, both in words and deeds. Some people find it difficult to openly discuss what they need, like or dislike about sex. Embarrassing? Maybe. Like the Marines say, "Is this the hill you want to die on?" Get over it! Look at where the embarrassment comes from. Your past? Mom said this or Dad said that. Move past it! Wouldn't you rather be a little embarrassed and discover a new source of sexual pleasure than to miss the opportunity and have regrets? Learn to share your sexual thoughts. For some this can take time. The more you openly discuss sex, the easier it becomes to share your innermost desires and needs with your love partner. Love thrives on truth. When you communicate the truth about how you feel, you increase the chances of keeping love alive and active.

Red Hot LoveNote. . . *For Men Only* ~ Impotence. Say the word and men cringe! This embarrassing disorder affects an estimated 30 million American males, but most of them prefer not to talk about it, let alone seek treatment. Impotency usually strikes men between the ages of 50 and 70. Among the leading causes of impotence are diabetes, heart disease, untreated hypertension, elevated cholesterol and cigarette smoking. Testosterone level low? Could be. Medical doctors often can do something about that. Making love can still be an exciting event, even without intercourse, if you both are free enough to use your imagination! By the way, impotency happens to the best of us occasionally. Unless it happens "all the time," there is usually nothing to be concerned about. Unless there is a medical problem, for most men, getting an erection is mostly in their mind. See your doctor. It's nothing to be ashamed of. Talking openly with your love partner about it also might help. It is a sign of strength, not weakness. Neither partner must ever talk about the problem while making love. That is sure death for a potentially healthy erection. Talk about it outside of the bedroom. You should have alternative plans when you do not get or maintain an erection. Perform foreplay with the understanding that intercourse is not the goal but that pleasure is. Give yourself permission to make love and be soft. Making love is not necessarily about intercourse, erections and orgasm. Most men think it is. Most women know better! To her, making love is holding, caressing, touching, tasting, rubbing, kissing, fondling, licking, massaging, being massaged and more. Be a student of foreplay! Let go of having to be hard for lovemaking to be good. Sexual anxiety, i.e., the pressure to perform, can often be a cause of impotency. Remember . . . an erection is caused by blood flow, and the main ingredient of blood is water. I suggest that you drink at least 8 glasses a day. If you know you will be making love, drink one or two glasses about an hour or so before lovemaking time. And finally, alcohol kills male performance as effectively as anything. Teach your lover to appreciate you for who you are. Teach her to be okay that you are soft AND you are still there for her, doing what you can to give pleasure by making love with her. While it may be a little frustrating for you, if you use your imagination, she will be pleased with your performance. And you may be amazed at how your ability to perform improves. Anything is possible if you believe it is! Let go of your attachment to having to be hard. It takes no strength to let go, only courage. What have you got to lose? What if it worked? What if IT worked?

Red Hot LoveNote. . . There is no such thing as a natural born lover. Learning how to make extraordinary love is something that takes practice. People who want their sex lives to be great are most likely happy to hear this. Learn more. Do more. Have more fun. Take your sexuality to new heights. There is always something new to learn about sex. That something new always feels good. Discover things together. Making love is a lot more fun that way.

Red Hot LoveNote. . . *For Men Only* ~ Not every woman screams your name in delight, rolls her eyes and causes the headboard to shake during sex. If she doesn't, it doesn't mean anything. She may be enjoying herself more than you think. Encourage her to express her pleasure in words you can understand. Let her know how it excites you to hear words like: "Ooooooh!" and "Oh! Yes! That's it! Harder!" It can tell you that what you are doing, she is enjoying. Tell her how hearing her lightly moan with pleasure encourages you to give that area more focus. Communicate. Orally and otherwise.

Red Hot LoveNote. . . Unresolved conflict paralyzes togetherness; it keeps you from connecting sexually and in all other ways. When issues arise, many couples focus on "WHO did what?" Blame never fully resolves anything; it keeps you stuck. Staying away from this type of impasse is much easier than getting out of it once you become entangled in it. Mature love partners who are committed to open and honest communications focus on "WHAT went wrong?" They talk without throwing zingers at each other. They listen with understanding and acceptance. They discuss healthy solutions and immediately put them into practice.

Red Hot LoveNote. . . Shape up your sex life. Work out. It will improve your endurance. Body image contributes to sexual energy as well as self-esteem. When you are in touch with your body, you are more inclined to see what it can do. Stamina is important to a satisfying sexual experience. Shape up or slip out. Some people report being exceptionally horny following a long workout. Exercise and practice improves almost all sexual performance. Taking care of yourself makes you feel younger! A great gift idea, one that may enhance your sex life, would be to give your lover and yourself a gift certificate to a health club. This is something else you can do together.

Red Hot LoveNote. . . *For Men Only* ~ Orgasm and ejaculation are two different things! Orgasm is defined as the climax of sexual excitement. You know what ejaculation is. For some of you, that IS orgasm. Try this: the next time you are making love, focus only on orgasm for her, without ejaculating. Push for as much sexual excitement as you can without purposely ejecting any fluid. This may take all the will power you have, but do it. Put HER satisfaction above your own and watch what happens. Let her know your goal is for her to achieve orgasm if she chooses, and next time it can be your turn. Her most responsive sexual organ is her brain. You must accept that her ultimate sexual satisfaction begins there. She needs to experience what making love is like, not just having sex! Most women are capable of achieving multiple orgasms during a lovemaking session. If your woman is not experiencing this type of pleasure with you and would like to, you must discover new ways of giving her pleasure. Putting her pleasure FIRST is a great place to begin! (. . . and all the women said, "Amen!")

Larry James

Red Hot LoveNote. . . Stage your very own "lick 'n' taste" fest! Gently smear your partner's body with thick, creamy, mildly warm chocolate. Pretend it is body paint. It's delicious. Take turns. Enjoy the taste of your lover in more ways than one. Get decadent. If you are worried about calories, you are missing the point!

Red Hot LoveNote. . . For sex to be great . . . become a teacher. Learn all you can from books, audio and video cassettes and seminars. Check out the recommended book list in the back of this book for some possibilities. Learn from loving your love partner freely and from mutually acceptable experimentation. Be a willing understudy. (Pun intended!)

Red Hot LoveNote. . . *For Women Only* ~ One of the reasons it is wise not to withhold in the sexual area is because when you say what you want, you can have so much more fun being with your partner sexually. Maybe you think your love partner knows what you want, and he really doesn't. What if what you wanted was okay with him? Perhaps you were nearing orgasm and he stopped too soon, and he didn't know. This is another peek at the open and honest part of your relationship. Open yourself up to your lover. Be courageous enough to be vulnerable. Tell him. You may not always get what you want, *and* you may be surprised . . . you very well may. You must always do your best to not have any expectations about whether your love partner will respond like *you* think he should. What this may mean is that you get to enjoy him the way he is and he gets to enjoy you the way you are while making love. Either way, you both win. It's called sexual freedom to be who you need to be for yourself, and at the same time, you get to be who you really are with your lover. That's what making love is all about: Sexual energy mutually exchanged, a sort of spiritual mingling. When you are always being honest about your innermost feelings you really can have more fun in bed.

Red Hot LoveNote. . . Have agreements about talking openly about sex and watch that part of your relationship spiral higher and higher. In the absence of agreement there is only confusion. Confusion gets in the way of a healthy sexual experience. Candidly discuss your attitudes, needs, likes and dislikes. It is your lover you are having this conversation with. Let that person know what you feel. How is someone to know if you don't say anything? Never expect your partner to read your mind. Often we withhold and wonder why the sexual part of our relationship isn't working as well as we think it should. Have an agreement to talk about sex. Have an agreement to make suggestions about adding variety to your sex life. Have an agreement to never criticize your lover . . . only offer ways to make things better. Have an agreement to not take personally anything that is said. Just know that your lover is expressing feelings and when it comes to feelings, no one is wrong. Choose to have spoken agreements about how often you like to make love and where you make love. Once you experience the turn-on you will both experience from the spoken words you have only thought about, you will wonder why you didn't agree to talk about making love long before you did. Speak your wants and needs!

Red Hot LoveNote. . . Anticipation is often an outgrowth of advance planning. Anticipate what you will do when you get together on Friday night (and it's only Tuesday morning). Anticipation is the beginning of foreplay; it sets the stage. When you anticipate, your imagination works overtime. It brings back feelings you experienced as a child. You hear yourself say, "I can hardly wait!" You begin to think about what it will be like to be with your love partner the next time you make love. You may even reach a point where you become so turned on, you temporarily take care of that need yourself, knowing that it will be even better when you and your lover get together.

Red Hot LoveNote. . . *For Men Only* ~ If you are truly interested in improving your sex life, remember this: "Foreplay begins with taking out the garbage without being asked!" You must be willing to give your partner what she needs on a practical and emotionally level. This means connecting with her emotionally outside of the bedroom, in ways that she needs. She needs to hear you say, "I love you." She needs to be appreciated; to hear that the house looks great after she's spent all day cleaning; to hear that she is still beautiful to you. She needs to see you "take the initiative" and share in the responsibilities of the home, including the household chores. She needs you to notice her new hairdo; to pick up the kids after soccer practice. It is easy to couple with someone emotionally for the time it takes to have sex. But what about foreplay? What about making love? Foreplay isn't just removing clothing so that you can have sex. Foreplay is doing whatever your lover needs to feel ready to make love. Most often it has more to do with how she is treated outside the bedroom than inside it.

Red Hot LoveNote. . . One of the keys to extraordinary sexual satisfaction is sexual know-how! Sexual ability is not something you inherently know. There are skills that can be developed together. Half of the fun and enjoyment of making love is learning how . . . together. Satisfying sex is one of the most rewarding aspects of our humanity. Reaching orgasm is one of the most powerful pleasures. Experiment. Talk about what feels good! No one knows everything there is to know about making love. All bodies are different; they respond differently. Explore. Together you can enjoy the opportunity to experience the potential of the sexual experience by understanding what your partner really wants and needs. And you must be courageous enough to discuss it!

Red Hot LoveNote. . . Anything is okay and is not perverted if you both are in agreement and it gives each of you pleasure. It is exciting to break from sexual routine. Vary positions. Find new places to make love. Watch a sexy movie. Experiment with sex toys. Discover the sexual limits you both have of giving pleasure to each other. Too much of the same way of making love can become boring. It may be wise to not immediately reject your partner's suggestion without giving it some thought. Take time to get used to the idea and to work on overcoming any inhibitions you may harbor. It is your choice. It must be your partner's commitment to honor it. Nothing is too kinky if it is a mutually agreeable and exhilarating experience for all. Never do anything together that you do not both enjoy!

Red Hot LoveNote. . . *For Men Only* ~ What happens after making love is very consequential to your love partner. It is equally important to kiss, caress, fondle and touch *after* you have made love, too. For most women, this is probably most important. Your partner can experience some of her most intimate moments after sex. In those moments she feels safe and secure. Hold her. Kiss her. Stroke her hair and her body. This is the after-glow. While this may not feel so important to you, it is extremely essential for her complete satisfaction. Placing a high priority on this time together can cause making love together to be more meaningful for each of you. If the first words out of your mouth after making love are, "Could you pick the kids up after their soccer game tomorrow?" or worse yet, you roll over and go to sleep, it has a tendency to cool her down instantly. She then knows that for you, it was "just sex" and not making love. Stay alert to her needs before, during and after making love.

Red Hot LoveNote. . . We are often victimized by our memory of past sexual encounters. If there was a time in your life (perhaps in your present relationship) when making love was a chore, where it was unfulfilling and just plain boring, most likely there were problems in your relationship that were showing up in the bedroom. That was then, this is now! Let go of being the victim. It doesn't look good on you. Acknowledge the experience. Accept it. Take responsibility for your share of the problems, forgive yourself and begin to reinvent a sexual relationship that frees your sexual soul and gives you power over the past.

Red Hot LoveNote. . . There is always a more appropriate time to discuss your concerns about your love-making sessions than when you are making love. You must never complain about or criticize your love partner's performance during or immediately after making love. That is not the right time! Words like: "I don't turn you on like I used to, do I?" or "How come you can't get it up like you used to? We used to make love for hours!" can cause passion to evaporate as quickly as the words are spoken. Often this kind of inquiry expresses your own self-doubts and may have little to do with your love partner. It also may be a signal that something is missing. It may be a request for tender words from the other partner. If you continue to have these feelings, they must be expressed. Choose a time, other than when you are making love, a time when things are going well, when the two of you can have an intimate conversation about the things that are most important to you.

Red Hot LoveNote. . . *For Women Only* ~ Just because a man loves you does not mean he has a crystal ball! Parents learned to intuitively know what you want. Mommy and daddy are no longer with you. You must actively communicate your needs. Never expect him to know what you want or need. If you want good lovin' – like something from the oven . . . hot and delicious – then be courageous and tell him what you need.

Red Hot LoveNote. . . *For Men Only* ~ Watch for the moods of your lover. When you look for signals you can almost always tell when your lover needs the comfort of your arms. Touch is important in a relationship, more so than you might imagine. Give her an unexpected, warm, body hug. Embrace the whole body. Make it a melting hug, one that gives you the sense of melting into each other. Don't let go until she does. Cherish the moment. Know that if it feels good to you, it feels good to her too. Breathe together. Establish a steady love rhythm; one that puts you in sync. Hold her close enough to feel her heartbeat. Feel, *really* feel the closeness of being together in this way. Listen for words of love expressed by touch. Hugging matters. It is therapeutic. Give in to the moment. Do not hurry this experience. When you are both in tune with each other, you experience a familiarity that most couples only dream about. A specific intention to surrender in this special way helps to keep the feeling of romance alive.

Red Hot LoveNote. . . Avoid selective sharing. When you are talking about making love with your love partner, share what is really in your heart. Say what you want. Have an agreement to listen without judgment. The agreement must include the right to not participate in something you consider not right for you, but without making a big deal out of it or criticizing your lover for speaking what he or she would like to try. Just say no. Or say, "Yes! Let's try that!" It may be difficult at first to share your sexual desires, but remember, each time you do, it will not only give you more freedom to naturally express what you want, most likely it will also be an incredible turn-on for your lover. Talking about making love with someone you love and being authentic about your desires is verbal foreplay.

Red Hot LoveNote. . . Variety is the spice of a healthy sexual appetite! Have a rendezvous in the middle of the night. Plan it. Talk about how it would be for one of you to wake up and begin to make love to your partner. Expect it to happen and when it does, be ready to respond. Anticipate how you will feel when your lover makes the move. What a turn-on! If you are worried about sleep, you are missing the point. You can sleep when you are dead! This is now. Be available to every opportunity to make love when the feeling is right and there is agreement between the two of you. You can feel your relationship grow!

Red Hot LoveNote. . . *For Men Only* ~ Never get on just to get off and then roll over. It may test you a bit to become a lingering lover, one who basks with your lover in the afterglow. Know this. Women want intimacy, the kind of intimacy that is more than in and out! There is a strong need to know she is loved, to be wanted. She wants to be your very special lover. She knows this when you take the time to cuddle after making love. She knows this when you pause to touch her where she wants to be touched. A brief and gentle shoulder rub or softly running your fingers through her hair in a very intimate gesture lets her know, too. Tell her you love her. Whisper that being in a committed relationship with her is the most incredible experience you have ever had. Put how you feel in your own words and speak them aloud. Never just roll over and go to sleep. That is always a mistake. It always will be. After you have made love it is infinitely wiser to spend some time with her. It's true that actions often speak louder than words. Be an active demonstration of who you are for her in your relationship. Lie beside her, spent. Hold her. Stay. *Be* with her. When she speaks, really give her your undivided attention. Listen. Fall asleep in each other's arms. "Wham! Bam! Thank you, Ma'am!" doesn't work! It never will. Never fall asleep without saying, "I love you."

Red Hot LoveNote. . . In a Shoebox Greetings card, the tiny little division of Hallmark, I read, "A relationship between a man and a woman is like a building. It needs a solid foundation. That 'foundation' cannot be sex alone. But sex can be the roof and several of the rooms, most of the hallway. The entire basement can be sex! The garage? Sex! The sidewalks and the driveway – sex, sex, sex! The lawn and most of the fence! The sky above the building! The . . ." Get the point? Making love is the ultimate connection between a woman and a man. It is the supreme letting go of everything, except the moment. It's when you can choose to really be with your love partner. Sex is an important part of a relationship. "But," you say, "I'm different! I have no feelings for my partner and making love with him/her is a waste of time. He/she is a cold fish," etc., etc., etc., or in other words, "Blah! Blah! Blah!" Don't kid yourself. When

continued

you get rid of the idea that "no sex" is someone else's fault and accept responsibility for your own, very personal, sexual self, you might find that a cold fish might warm up to that. All sorts of things can happen. It's like you create this enormous freedom and now you can express yourself in ways you had never imagined. When you love someone, I mean, really love someone, making love is not only the garage, the sidewalks and the driveway, it's the sky overhead! To borrow an old phrase: It becomes you. It truly becomes you. Not only that, it becomes you to be who you are sexually. To mutually explore the wonderful world of making love with – not to – each other, can lead to some incredibly brilliant discoveries. Making love is important to every relationship; it is the ultimate way of expressing how much you love someone.

Red Hot LoveNote. . . To add a little extra excitement in your day, try an "afternoon delight." Plan a brief, intimate rendezvous to have a quickie during the lunch hour. It may be exciting to discover that you enjoy getting connected other than only after dark. Make it on the kitchen table, do it on the floor in the bathroom, or on a blanket in the sunlight of the back yard. Be creative. Planning such an event together will surely create anticipation. Just the thought of being together, if for but a few short moments, can give you both a renewed energy to continue the day. Who knows what the evening can bring forth?

Red Hot LoveNote. . . *For Women Only* ~ Men love women who love to make love! Don't just lie there! He can have that much fun with an inflatable doll. Show him you get pleasure from sex, too! Actively pursue him sexually. Never let him do all the work. Make the first move! Make love to *him*. Taking turns can be FUN!

Red Hot LoveNote. . . Beautiful comes in all shapes and sizes. There is no known documented case of a man ever admitting he married an ugly woman. The same is true for women. Ugly is an interpretation. Beauty is only skin deep. Hello!! Get to know your body. Look at it. All of it! Accept it or do something to make it different. Look at it in the mirror. Study it. Say "hello" to the beautiful you! That's you looking back at you. Say aloud, "I love you, body!" Watch yourself smile. When you can love what you look like and who you are, the love you have to share becomes more readily available to the one you are with. Accept that you are a beautiful creature of God and that you love YOU!

Red Hot LoveNote. . . Communication is paramount for a great relationship to demonstrate great sex! There can be no *great sex* without exciting and sometimes erotic conversation. Talking about sex can be almost as stimulating at the act itself. I said *almost!* Suggestion: Begin by saying something like, "Remember the other night when you put your hand between my legs and whispered 'I love to touch you there?' That really turned me on." It is much easier to invent new ways of being sexual with your love partner when you are both in a creative conversation about it . . . together. Try it.

Red Hot LoveNote. . . *For Men Only* ~ A woman can have intercourse – if she chooses – without being aroused. A man cannot. A popular myth among men is that you *must* have an orgasm if you are aroused or you will suffer physical pain. Temporary discomfort? Perhaps. In plain language you can understand: "Blue Balls" is a myth! Given time, your urge to have orgasm will simply disappear. If you must, you can relieve the tension of the moment by masturbation. Never do anything to cause her to feel guilty or to be afraid to say, "No." When she says "No," it is important for you to understand that she is rejecting the invitation to have sex, not you! A woman under pressure to have sex will get no pleasure from it and may eventually come to resent you and the act itself. Give her a warm and tender embrace and tell her you love her. Never pull back or withhold physical affection – hugs and kisses – even though she may not be in the mood for love. People have different sexual appetites. Honor them.

Red Hot LoveNote. . . When it comes to relationships, the shortest distance between two points is not a straight line. Every couple has their ups and downs. The secret is to work through your difficulties as rapidly as you can so you can get to the good stuff. It is not wise to allow petty differences to interrupt the time necessary to provide sexual pleasure for each other. When two people love each other, it is natural for them to want to make love with each other in very special ways. To allow anything to get in the way of this process keeps you from enjoying the freedom to sexually express your love for each other. Work diligently to make the ups and downs go as smoothly as humanly possible so you can enjoy each other in bed or wherever the mood strike you.

Red Hot LoveNote. . . *For Women Only* ~ If you find that orgasms are easy to achieve during masturbation and virtually nonexistent during intercourse, ask your lover to tease and please you while you are making love. After considerable foreplay, begin masturbating until you feel you are about to reach orgasm, then allow your partner to enter you while you continue to masturbate. For most men just knowing that you are uninhibited enough to help yourself to ecstasy in this way is a red hot turn-on. This could be the time to celebrate simultaneous orgasms with your love partner. Picture this: two lovers, sexually alive, writhing in ecstasy as your mutual orgasms surge to a powerful crescendo. Orgasmic unison can only lead to a very wet conclusion. The greatest orgasmic success can be reached when you feel most secure with your own sexuality and with a partner you trust. It is okay to play with fire in the bedroom! Making love is an honest expression of how you feel toward each other. Set off some fireworks!

Red Hot LoveNote. . . Learn to carefully choose your moods. Consistently attending to a bad mood can be highly destructive to your relationship. It can kill sexual desire. Quickly get to the root of the problem by looking in the mirror. Learning to take responsibility for your individual moods is a high priority if you want your sexual life to be something you are proud to participate in. Learn to roll with the punches. Be okay with the way things turn out. Let go of your resentments. This does not mean you should hide from anger to keep from being afraid. Resentment is often the offspring of anger. Often the moods you create come from fear. Accept responsibility that fear is only as bad as you can imagine it to be. Face what you fear. Fear can never prevail against love. Courage is the impetus of its demise. You've heard of "being in the mood." Be in the mood that complements your relationship. Be in the mood that empowers you and your love partner to never again be afraid of who is going to show up when he or she walks into the room. Can you imagine how it would feel to live with someone and never know what kind of a mood he or she is going to be in when you see them? Can you imagine that this could close a lot of doors? Opportunity for sexual enlightenment lies on the other side of those doors. You must never allow yourself to hide from the truth – the truth of being afraid, of being sad, of being happy, of being bored, of being resentful, angry or any other feeling. Feelings are real *and* we can learn that paying attention to the moods we live in, the ones that suggest our feelings, can significantly alter our relationships. Choose your moods carefully. Be sensitive to how they can affect your relationship. Do they support you, your love partner and the relationship?

Red Hot LoveNote. . . *For Men Only* ~ Kissing can improve the overall level of intimacy you experience with your love partner; not only sexual intimacy. It is a sensual pleasure meant to be enjoyed. A kiss can bring lovers together. A kiss can make her lips hum. A kiss should not always be used as a prelude to making love. Women love to be kissed, held and appreciated for who they are. Tonight . . . surprise your partner with a warm, passionate kiss, then speak those words every woman loves to hear, "I love you, baby! You're the best!"

Red Hot LoveNote. . . When preparing to make love, dress appropriately. For her . . . there are some clothes she can wear only for sex. Visit a Victoria's Secret, Frederick's of Hollywood or similar store for ideas. For him . . . some women like the feel of silk boxer shorts. Clothes can be a turn-on and are to be taken off. Most people make love naked. Many sleep in the buff. Part of the fun of making love is the casting off of clothes and preparing to couple. Take it slow. Be intentional. Begin to remove a piece of clothing, change your mind and move to something else. Tease. Keep your lover in suspense. Help each other. Take turns. Be creative. Disrobing can be an erotic adventure. Begin to make love before there is a heap of clothes in the middle of the floor. Do it differently this time.

Red Hot LoveNote. . . Allow the bedroom to be a con-
tinual training ground for making love. Get rid of the TV.
Choose some soft music, the kind with no distracting
words. Place real flowers on the nightstand. Make it a
playground for great sex! Light some candles. Toss some
scented body power on satin sheets to introduce a fresh
feeling to the playing field. Practice making love. Practice
does not make you perfect, it only makes you better.
Stretch yourself beyond what is comfortable. Enjoy each
other. One of the secrets of great sex is giving!

Red Hot LoveNote. . . *For Women Only* ~ Often it is difficult to find the right words to tell your partner you are not in the mood for sex without causing him to feel rejected. Reassuring your mate that you are rejecting the invitation for having sex rather than rejecting him is important. "Not tonight, dear – I have a headache" is a copout. If you don't feel in the mood . . . say so. It's okay. You don't have to give a phony reason. Phony reasons are identifiable. They are noticed and filed away. They sound like putoffs. Too many of them and you will find your lover cooling off. Once you learn to openly communicate your sexual needs and desires and reach agreement about how you can say "No" in a way he can accept, the more he will trust you and love you and the less he will feel rejected.

Red Hot LoveNote... It increases your pleasure to lounge around in the moment as long as you can without going over the edge. Exercise self-control. When you feel you are nearing orgasm, slow down . . . linger in the moment. Feel it. Think about it. Experience it. Begin again. Do what feels good. Speed up. Slow down. Take your time. Start once more. The longer you allow sexual energy to circulate in your body, the more powerfully you can experience the pleasure and fulfillment of a deliberate, intentional, explosive orgasm.

Red Hot LoveNote. . . The so-called shame of masturbation runs deep for many of us. Get over it! Hair will
not grow on the palm of your hand and you will not go
blind! There is nothing wrong with taking care of yourself sexually when your love partner is unavailable or if
you feel you need immediate sexual release. Almost everyone masturbates occasionally, but seldom do we talk about
it. Many who would lie about this would lie about other
things too! Until you know how to pleasure yourself, it
is very difficult to tell your love partner how to give you
the pleasure you need. Self-stimulation is one of the very
best ways to discover your sexual responsiveness. In a
healthy love relationship it is okay to talk about "taking
care of yourself." Some sexually mature love partners often
help each other to reach orgasm by mutual masturbation
while making love. Once you break through this barrier,
you can discover an intimacy so profound that every area
of your relationship is enhanced beyond belief. Some
lovers agree to masturbate their partner when they are not
"in the mood" for intercourse. It is just another way of
experiencing sexual pleasure together. It was George
Carlin who said, "If God didn't want us to masturbate,
he would have made our arms shorter!"

Red Hot LoveNote. . . *For Men Only* ~ When you make love, get your senses involved. Touch your lover's skin with your tongue. Is it warm? Slick? Wet? Sticky? Soft? Pay attention to taste. Salty? Sweet? Listen for sounds that say you are being enjoyed. Did that soft whimper tell you you are doing something right? Watch your lover. When you do what you are doing, does she close her eyes? Does her body move slowly to the rhythm of the music or rise to meet your touch? What scents have you become aware of? Intercourse is only a small part of making love. Her skin is very sensitive to your touch. Take into account all of your five senses to more fully enjoy lovemaking. Never rush sex, unless you have mutual agreement for a quickie. Gypsy Rose Lee once said, "Anything worth doing is worth doing slowly." Think fast. Go slow.

Red Hot LoveNote. . . When is it okay for you to say "Yes" to sex when you would really rather say "No"? Here is the answer: When love, tenderness, a concern for your partner or your own need for physical closeness feels right. It is only and always your choice. Making love in spite of the absence of physical desire hurts no one unless it is done because you would feel guilty or afraid to say no.

Red Hot LoveNote. . . In your private conversations about sex, be careful not to stray into the area of "sexual sarcasm." If you want to make love and your partner doesn't, be sensitive to the other person's needs. Saying words like: "You ALWAYS have a headache!" or "I suppose you're working late again at the office, huh?" or "You NEVER have time for me!" can only irritate and certainly never raise the level of sexual interest. You want to initiate, not irritate. Choose your words carefully. Think before you speak. Words, once spoken, do their intended damage. Remember, you cannot un-ring a bell.

Red Hot LoveNote. . . *For Men Only* ~ Not all men "love" performing cunnilingus. However, if you are one of those men, get over it! Most men can be extremely competent at this sexual skill. If you are NOT one of those men, you must learn this most delicious way of pleasuring your partner. Almost universally, women love to receive oral gratification and they strongly appreciate a man who can bring them to intense orgasms in this way. She must trust you to allow you to visit this area between her legs with your mouth and fingers. Take a shower together, then make love *to* her using only your tongue and your fingers. Begin with a lingering, passionate kiss on her lips. Then very slowly follow an irregular and purposeful path all over her body; kissing her breasts, first one and then the other, until you reach the target zone. Approach this area slowly. Most women love to be teased. The inner part of her thigh is her most tender spot. Kiss it. Create anticipation. Bathe it with your tongue, make designs on it. Come close, then move away. Tease her. Nestle her pubic hair. Gently touch

continued

her there with wet fingers. The best lubricant is saliva. Slowly spread her legs wider with your hands. Focus all of your energy on giving her the gift of the talents of your tongue. Gently, and as she becomes more aroused, pull back the folds of her skin and kiss her, softly, then harder. Make love to her with your mouth. Go with her. If she lifts her body toward you or moves away with the tension of her rising orgasm, move with her. Keep your hot mouth upon her. Practice hands-on love; let your fingers say, "I love you" without words. Don't stop until she gives you a signal. Most men often stop too soon. Women plummet back to square one if you do. Hang in there for the duration. A woman can stay excited for up to a full hour after she's had an orgasm. Caution: Beware of instant replays. You must be respectful of her need to have time and space between each orgasm if she wants you to continue. After orgasm, her clitoris feels tender. Let her tell *you* when to begin again, slow down, speed up, be more gentle, or apply more pressure. This is the forbidden kiss she will treasure!

Red Hot LoveNote. . . Touching with a slow hand can instill a tenderness that has the capacity to integrate the body and soul and stimulate our partner to a quieter, longer-lasting orgasm. Concentrating only on touch causes us to slow down. We must learn to have reverence for the miracle of touch. Use it to engage in a way of making love that nurtures our partner. A slower, softer touching of your lover's body exhibits respect for the person, and for the very act of making love. A gentle, sexual joining in the slow lane is more deliberate, intentional, focused and hot! It encourages sexual harmony.

Red Hot LoveNote. . . There is nothing more romantic than a marriage in which the spark still flickers and, more importantly, ignites on a regular basis. Just because you are married does not mean you have to stop acting like lovers. Passion does not stay alive by itself. Neither does love. A garden unattended does not explode into color; it withers and dies. Love and passion must be nurtured. If you expect love and passion to continue to burn as an unattended fire, you will both burn out. Commitment most be renewed. Love must be rekindled. The true romantics are those who continually work together to maintain the love and passion that brought them together in the first place. While the pursuit is exciting and fun in the beginning, the responsibility each partner has of investing time and energy to supporting a healthy and prosperous marriage on a continuing basis is undeniably more important than hoping that things work out while giving far less effort than you spent on winning your partner's hand. Holding on to it is the key. Once married, there is more at stake. So why would you pay less attention to your lover's needs once the prize has been won? The bonding of two hearts continues long after marriage. It takes diligent effort and a committed love for you to continue to stir the sparks and keep the fire burning. Getting married is just the beginning.

Red Hot LoveNote. . . *For Women Only* ~ Making love is very important to a man. It makes him feel wanted. If you do not feel like making love, it is okay to say no to sex, but make sure you say yes to loving him. Sex is acceptance for a man. It is a primal urge. When he suggests sexual intimacy, it is important for you to receive him in some way whether you choose to have sex with him or not. Men do not take sexual rejection very well. Hold him close. Let him know you will make love another time, but right now you only want to feel him close to you. A man will often have a tough time accepting that it is not HIM you are rejecting. It is important for you to know this. Demonstrate your love and affection for him in other ways to reassure him. Both of you may take sexual rejection personally when it is a reflection of some tension between the two of you. Men also love women who love to make love. If you enjoy having sex with him, this is the moment he needs to hear it.

Red Hot LoveNote. . . Music and candles create a mood. When you want to become sexually intimate, you want the mood to be warm and mellow, soft and romantic. Place a few scented candles around the room. If you can place one or two candles in front of a mirror, do so. Watch how the flicker of the candles adds to the seductive view you have of your lover while you are making love. Notice the shadows two lovers create . . . on the sheets . . . on the wall. Carefully choose the music that will most enhance your experience of each other. Select music without words, music that will not distract from the ambiance of the moment.

Red Hot LoveNote. . . When love partners have a great sexual relationship, they are more likely to do their best to work through their problems. Relationship problems always show up in the bedroom. Ann Landers once said, "If your relationship is on the rocks, the rocks are usually in the mattress." You can turn that rocky mattress into a deserted, white sandy beach where you can openly and honestly communicate your sexual needs; it can become a place where lovers meet to make love and share their bodies with one another.

Red Hot LoveNote. . . *For Men Only* ~ Have fun with sex. Call her from the office and ask her if she would like to play doctor. Tell her how anxious you are to make a house call. Think hot! Wear a stethoscope and one of those funny little scrub aprons. Have your sex toys be your examining instruments. Talk doctor. Remind her that "the doctor always knows best" and you are only interested in her well-being. A good "love doctor" never asks the patient where it hurts . . . he asks, "Where does it feel good?" Give your lover a prescription, a description of what is to come. "Prep" together by showering together. If you can find one, dress her in one of those gowns the doctor gives you while you are waiting in the examining room. You know, the one that flaps open in the back. It's called easy access. Tell her the dining room table is your gurney . . . or the picnic table in the back yard . . . or the flatbed of your pickup. Several thick and fluffy blankets will make it nice and cushiony. Offer her the cure for sexual boredom: making deliberate, wanton, passionate love. Demonstrate your most erotic bedside manner. Have fun with sex. It doesn't have to be only humping without words! Find her funny spot. Make her giggle! It's okay to laugh and have some fun while you are making love. It is written: Laughter doeth good like a medicine. Make love. Tell her she is "just what the doctor ordered"! *Be* someone the patient can enjoy; be her good medicine. This one is for her! Surprise her with a session of making love that will take her far beyond all of her expectations! Variety is the spice you may need to have extraordinary hot sex. Make your next appointment for another house call. Or next time, she can play nurse!

Red Hot LoveNote. . . Great sex is never boring. When it's great, you rarely become weary of it. It doesn't have to be every night for you to experience the wonders of the ultimate closeness. It can be great whenever you do it, once a week, twice a week or three times a month. Whenever you make love . . . passionately make love! *Be* in the moment. Put all you have into it. Do your very best not to be distracted by your everyday happenings. It's not how often, it's whether it feels good when you do it. Be gentle, be a little less than gentle, be sexually romantic, be however you need to be for making love to be experienced as "making love," not just having sex. Variety is also one of the keys to avoiding boredom. Sex only becomes boring when you have little desire in making love with the one you love or if you always do it the same way. Promise yourself never to settle for anything less than giving it your best . . . whenever the mood strikes you!

Red Hot LoveNote. . . Experiment with conversation as a sexual turn-on. Talk openly about sex. What makes *you* feel good? Whisper what *you* like in your lover's ear. The more you can express yourself in whispers that communicate love, passion and the excitement you are looking for with your love partner, the more you increase your anticipation level about making love. It's called "foreplay with words."

Red Hot LoveNote. . . *For Women Only* ~ Want to create some excitement for your love partner? Make him a very personal and perhaps sexxxy home video. Rent a video camera. Set it up in a place that will cause him to recall fond memories when he views your video. It may be the bedroom, the back yard, or a familiar hotel room. Write a script. In your most sincere way, tell him how much you love him. Talk sexy. If he likes for you to dress or undress in a special way when you make love, dress or undress that way. Use your imagination. Surprise him with something you have always wanted to say and were afraid to say face to face. You know what he likes. Push it to the limits. If you dare, give it an "X" rating. Not only is it likely to turn your lover on, it also may turn you on in the process. If you are feeling really bawdy (and brave), invite him to watch or ask him to be the producer/director.

Red Hot LoveNote. . . What about lack of desire for sex? Always remember, making love is necessary to demonstrate the closeness that love partners NEED to know they are loved. Men and women experience sexual desire differently. Testosterone in a man is an aggressive hormone, while estrogen in a woman is a more passive hormone. It's difficult to distract a man from sex. A man has more conscious thoughts about sex than a woman and often has the physical evidence to prove it. A woman can become easily distracted. Her mood can change quickly with the sound of a baby crying, the "tone" rendered in misunderstandings or a repetitive thought of something yet to do that crosses her mind. When you were first together there was romantic love: discovery, newness, desire, excitement and anticipation. Real love is not characterized by desire. In time, both partners come to accept the reality that real love is a willingness to be together, to be close,

continued

to often come together regardless of their desire to do so. It is a wise partner – man and woman – who initiates sex in spite of a lack of desire for it. It establishes a presence for love to express itself. It offers evidence that you love each other and want to be close. Desire fades when lovers become lazy in the romance department. For romance to be present, it must be created over and over again. Do sexy things that create a sensual environment for making love and the feelings will follow. When both love partners understand that between a man and a woman there are differences that you may never fully understand, you can then put aside your dissimilarities and begin to focus on loving your partner in ways that honor that person for who he or she is. It helps you get on with the business of having a healthy love relationship, one that routinely transcends a lack of desire for sex.

Red Hot LoveNote. . . Introduce a Red Hot game to your boudoir. The object of the game is to make love without having intercourse. It is each partner's choice to reach orgasm. Set a date you can both look forward to. Rent a hotel suite if you must to avoid any interruptions. Begin with no distractions. Plan ahead. Bring your bedroom toys. Light some fragrant candles. Enjoy some chilled wine and warm conversation. Have a bath or shower together. Get to know your lover's body. Arrange for your favorite music. Take turns giving pleasure with your fingers, mouth, tongue, or favorite toy. Use your imagination. Play. Make sure you have oils for a long, leisurely, and very thorough massage. Take your time. Enjoy touching each other. Delight in the journey to steamy, passionate sex. The goal is mutual satisfaction. Agreeing to an evening of making love without intercourse takes the pressure to perform away. This mutual understanding causes you to focus on helping your lover reach orgasm without penile penetration. Savor your lover's body. Sex is fun and pleasure is good for you!

Red Hot LoveNote. . . *For Men Only* ~ It's fun to take turns making love to each other. Tonight only make love to her. Your turn will be some other time. Only focus on giving her pleasure. Do whatever she wants. For this night, be her sex slave. Encourage her to communicate with words or actions what she wants. Add a little excitement to it by asking her to send a letter to your office about what she would like for you to do with her tonight! Forget about your own orgasm. There is always time for that next time (or you can take care of yourself later). Tonight it's her turn to have all of your sexual energy focused upon her.

Red Hot LoveNote. . . Anger is often an attempt to make someone feel guilty. That is a deadly game. It kills sexual desire. This does not mean that anger is bad. People do things and their partners choose to feel angry. We must deal with the feelings of anger to be complete with them. For men, holding on to anger can make it stay soft longer than necessary. For women, desire seems to disappear when anger presents itself. If we want our close encounters to be highly charged sexual experiences . . . we must work through our anger issues quickly.

Red Hot LoveNote. . . Whether it is tender or lusty, sex is first and foremost about self-expression, not performance or skills. Most women seem to enjoy the more gentle and tender approach to making love. Equally exciting is when you are both wildly self-absorbed in your own erotic sensations. The magic is balance. Sometimes you may feel the need to have wild, carried-away sex. At other times, you both may equally enjoy more intensely connected, soulful sex – lying together, passionately joined, with very little movement, simply enjoying your soulful union. You may reach a slow, purposeful orgasm, or you may not. Sexually mature love partners watch for silent messages, those signals that suggest the mood. They respect each other's wishes. Taking responsibility for establishing the mood you desire, whether wild or whimsical, is essential for making love great.

Red Hot LoveNote. . . *For Men Only* ~ After an evening of joyful lovemaking, it is important to continue to hold and touch each other. You have heard the stories about men who, after orgasm, fade fast. This is mostly true. Given the energy it requires, it is indeed tiring at best. However, if you want the sexual part of your love relationship to prosper, you must not be a victim of your own stupidity. The male orgasm should not be the conclusion of making love. If you love your love partner, remember it is always important for you to communicate that love to her, before, during and after sex. It lets her know that she is the most important person in your life . . . even when, totally spent, you would really rather roll over and go to sleep. You can also communicate without words. Holding, touching, and caressing says it all. Simply coming and then falling asleep will put the damper on future joyful sexual escapades. Cuddle. Hold her. Whisper that you love her. Don't just roll over. Feel what it is like to fall asleep in each other's arms.

Red Hot LoveNote. . . If your lover isn't performing like you think he or she should and you are in the process of making love, that is not the time to say so. First of all, think about this: "What expectation did you have that did not get fulfilled?" Non-performance may only be in the mind of the beholder. Acceptance is its own reward. To accept the love that is given in the manner in which it is given is a gift to the giver. If you want your lover to do something different, that person will never know unless you say something or lead the person in some sexy way to discover what *you* want. Consider that if you keep this to yourself, nothing will be different. Show them or tell them. When it feels good, always acknowledge your partner for *his* or *her* wonderful discovery. Express your enjoyment in a loving way.

Red Hot LoveNote. . . Do spoons! Spoons fit together. So do two people who love each other. You know. That time when you only cuddle. No sex. Only that warm and loving coming together . . . his front to your back . . . only holding each other in a close, body to body connection. Notice that perfect fit. Get really close. Pay attention to the love that is being expressed in this way. Feel your lover's heartbeat. Quietly spoken, romantic words as well as gentle caresses can add to this loving experience of each other.

Red Hot LoveNote. . . *For Women Only* ~ Be careful not to suggest to your love partner that because he can't get it up, there must be something wrong with you, i.e., that you do not turn him on like you used to. When a man is having trouble getting an erection or keeping it up, it is usually him, NOT YOU! The last thing he needs is something more to think about when he is doing the best he can. Talk about it later. There is nothing that can chill a hot time more than suggesting that something is wrong with what is going on in the moment. Save it. For now . . . tell him it's okay. Hold him. Accept what he can give. Cuddle. Don't take it personally. Every man has moments when what is supposed to work, doesn't. Often women do not understand this. Demonstrate your understanding by being patient. This may be the night you get to take care of yourself.

Red Hot LoveNote. . . When you make love, you bond on a mental, emotional and spiritual level. You experience a deep sense of acceptance, contribution, and receptivity. Giving yourself totally to your love partner is a gift of love more valuable than the physical act itself. It takes away the sense of being alone. Being fully connected with the one you love eliminates any vulnerability you might feel when you are completely, intimately and emotionally naked in the eyes of your partner. It suggests the greatest possible benefit with limited risk. The reward is in direct proportion to any exposure you may feel. When you move past this potential peril at the hands of a caring and thoughtful lover, the imminent bonding is ecstatic, memorable, emotionally and spiritually uplifting.

Red Hot LoveNote. . . *For Men Only* ~ If you find that you always lapse into lethargy after a romp in the sack no matter what you did that day, you are most likely getting signals from your body that it is time to get fit! After sex, it is normal for you to feel weak and very tired. Before ejaculation, there is an energetic and impulsive burst of energy. During ejaculation, there is a sudden and very intense release of tension, a natural tendency to feel deeply relaxed. The pelvic muscles become five to ten times more tense than normal when sexual arousal begins. After orgasm, the muscle tension drops rapidly to a level below where it began. Unless you always feel this way, it is not a problem . . . simply enjoy the afterglow with your partner as a way to slowly unwind together.

Red Hot LoveNote. . . A woman needs to feel loved to make love. Women need emotional support to be able to offer sexual release for a man. A man needs to make love to feel loved. Men need sexual release to be able to offer emotional support to women. Sexual communication is not only about expressing yourself. It is also about being received; being understood. Somewhere in between, there is balance. Negotiate. Offer to meet the other half way to get your needs and the needs of the relationship met. Learn to respect and honor the differences. Vive la différence?

Red Hot LoveNote. . . *For Men Only* ~ You NEED to know what women want. Your love partner needs to feel wanted. She doesn't want to be needed. She needs to be wanted, to feel connected to her partner. She wants someone who is a slow lover. Someone who takes his time; someone who makes love on purpose. She does not want or need a *two-minute wonder!* Be more on purpose and intentional. A woman wants to be more than a wife. She wants to be your best friend *and* your lover. She wants you to do things that cause her to feel like a woman . . . not a wife. She wants romance. Send her an occasional "warm fuzzy" greeting card for no special reason, not just when you need to say "I'm sorry" or want something. She wants lots of unexpected hugs and meaningful kisses. She wants an occasional breakfast in bed. Guess who gets to be Chef? She wants and needs time alone. Honor her space. And when she is with you, she wants everyone to know she is with YOU. She wants affection. She wants to know she is really loved. You may say, "She knows I love her!" This may be true AND she still needs to hear you say it. Be generous with speaking, "I love you." Your partner wants you to feel free to say what you *feel* . . . not what you think she needs to hear. A woman wants you to take time to talk about things that are important to her, regardless of whether YOU think they are important. She needs you to listen to what she is saying. Give her all your attention. She needs sincerity. She longs to be in the shelter of her lover's arms. She wants your time together to make her feel like she's been given a gift. And most of all, she wants and needs respect!

Red Hot LoveNote. . . The imagination is a powerful tool. It is a key ingredient to foreplay. We think words and our mind translates those words to mind pictures we can relate to. It may be a suggestion of an erotic moment you both shared in the past. It may be a new magic moment you are in the process of inventing. Words and imagination can be a massive turn-on. Often, with words, we can almost feel our lover touching us in our very favorite places.

Red Hot LoveNote. . . To paraphrase comedian Jerry Seinfeld, "Women need a reason to make love; men only need a place to have sex!" Perhaps there is a time for each bias. Some men feel that any position for sex is okay as long as her head doesn't block the TV. You will never receive the sexual satisfaction you need to connect on a far deeper level if you cannot be in the moment, having reasons and creating interesting places to make love . . . not just have sex! Making love requires sensitivity to the endeavor! It demands focus and purpose. Having sex is different than making love. Having only sex may give you the sexual release you need, but it lacks some of the main ingredients you need to maintain a healthy love relationship. Needing only a place to have sex doesn't communicate the kind of love a woman needs to have a reason to make love. Face it, they both bring pleasure of a different variety. However, it increases the odds of having your relationship work when you can give the majority of your most intimate moments together your undivided attention, expressing love in intentional, meaningful and loving ways. That's making love!

Red Hot LoveNote. . . Listen for what your lover wants when you are making love. Ask. It's okay! "Does that feel good? What would you like to try that you haven't tried?" Encourage your love partner to be open to talk about what he or she likes. Better yet, have agreements to tell each other by guiding the other person's hands to places you would like for them to discover. It's okay to talk about making love while you are making love. Pay attention to the details of desire. Make noises that tell your lover that what he or she is doing feels good. Explore new love-making positions. Try some love toys. We often make love to our love partner the way we would like them to make love to us. Watch for this. It may contain some important clues. It helps to have confirmation that what you are doing feels good and is something you should continue. Talk about making love when you are not in the mood and watch the mood shift.

Red Hot LoveNote. . . *For Women Only* ~ Initiate. Start sex with your lover sometime real soon! Be assertive. If your lover can handle it, be aggressive. Most men love it when their lover makes the first sexual overtures. For them it is a real turn-on. Talk to your man. Ask him if he would enjoy being awakened in the middle of the night to finish you off, assuming you have taken the initiative to start without him. Ask if he would like to know when you are *in the mood.* Discover what turns him on. Ask him what that is. You may be surprised! It really is okay for a woman to initiate sex whenever she is turned on and wants to make love. Talking about this in advance can also be a turn-on. It can be very beneficial when you have agreements about your spontaneity. Think about this. If you always already think you know what makes your man feel special when you are making love with him, you may never discover the other interesting possibilities that he may hold as sacred fantasies, fantasies you both might enjoy together. When you ask and he has the courage to tell you, you can surprise him by being the sexual gourmet he has always dreamed about.

Red Hot LoveNote. . . Interpretation and choice. Many
of us dwell only on the interpretation we make of a sexual situation, activity, or circumstance. The other option
seems clear. It is the choice we are destined to make about
it. Interpretation always and only comes from our experience of something from our past. We draw on our awareness of past feelings and emotions and make decisions with
prejudiced views, notions and opinions. It could be a sexual action or activity we felt was inappropriate or were
afraid to try because of our cultural or religious upbring-
ing. Choice comes from nowhere. To choose is to create.
New sexual choices, i.e., oral sex, mutual masturbation,
etc., create new possibilities. The courage to make new

choices is encouraged by the willingness to risk, to be vulnerable, to try something new with our lover rather than have our sexual togetherness become boring and dull by leaning only on the interpretation of what we THINK about something. The unwillingness to consider new options for exciting activities that sexually stimulate could mean we are committed to a sex life that is monotonous and ordinary. Any new experience can only come after we muster the courage to choose. Self-esteem is strengthened when we exercise courage. Courage offers us a boldness to explore. Interpretation can only restrict sexual exploration. Perhaps there are some mutually acceptable, new choices in your immediate future.

Red Hot LoveNote. . . It's morning. Your love partner is ready to leave for the office. You give her a warm hug and whisper in her ear, "Let's make love tonight. Are you up for the game?" This will give you both all day to think about it. Slip a Red Hot LoveNote in her briefcase. Call her at the office and give her a sexy reminder. Leave a message with her secretary, "Ask her to remember the game tonight! She will know which one!" Arrange in advance to have someone deliver a sexy card to the office. Go all out! Make this night the world series of sex! Get creative. Women can do this as well as men. Caution: There may be times when the game needs to be postponed because of stormy weather (i.e., the person has had a stressful day). Be okay with however it works out. Have agreements not to take it personally. If your lover comes home partly cloudy, you might assume several things: he or she had a bad day, is physically exhausted or just does not want to play. Conjuring up your own cloudy to partly cloudy forecast (what YOU think) to avoid the game is not okay. Also remember, if during the day you discover you are not up for the game, it is not wise to lead someone into thinking that you are and instead of saying so, you come home in a bad mood. That is the coward's way out. This can only cause suspicion and resentment to creep in. To put it another way, it is not being honest with yourself OR the one you love. Have courage enough to say what needs to be said. If you are not in the mood, you might say, "Let's plan on making love tomorrow evening. Okay?"

Red Hot LoveNote. . . You should never assume that your love partner knows what you need while making love. The solution is simple: Ask for what you need. Ignorance will keep you stuck. If you are too embarrassed to ask, talk about your embarrassment first and your needs second. Be patient. If it has been a long time since you talked, remember patience is a prerequisite. Do things that require no conversation. For example, agree that you will guide your lover's hand to a point that feels good. We assume that when people love us, they will automatically know what we need. Nothing could be further from the truth. This is fear rearing its ugly head. Fear builds resentment. It keeps you in bondage. It can immobilize the sexual desire in your relationship. You must ask for what you need! You are worthy of having the most incredible sex you can imagine. Believe it! Ask . . . and it shall be given. This assumes that you love each other and want the best from the relationship that is possible. If that's the case . . . ask.

Red Hot LoveNote. . . *For Men Only* ~ Carefully listen for clues to sexual accessibility. Women often try to tell us, without really telling us, that they would like for us to make love with them. We sometimes miss those clues. It's easy to miss those kinds of clues when someone is being too subtle and we are not paying attention. Nowhere is it written that a woman can't have a strong sexual drive, and at the same time face the same fear a man faces when he asks his lover if she would like to make love . . . the fear of sexual rejection. Encourage your lover to be brave and to do more than drop hints when she is turned on and ready to play. Then . . . pay attention. Remind her that subtlety is not a virtue. An occasional, "I'm horny. Do you want to mess around?" may not be too sexy but it makes the point. Be careful not to miss those points. Nor should

continued

you pass up the opportunity. You know how it is when you get rejected over and over again. Soon asking for it becomes a worrisome process. Then you tell yourself it's not worth the effort because she will only say no again. Miss these points and pass up the opportunity too often and she may become resigned that taking the risk, putting herself "out there," is just not worth it. It is easier to hear clues when you are listening for them. Have an agreement to help each other recognize the clues. Never play games. If you are horny, say so! You may not want to use those words *or* you might. The points are these. Have agreements and listen. Encourage your love partner to let you know when she wants to make love. And remember to hear what is being said. Oh, yes! And follow through. Make love.

Red Hot LoveNote. . . When your relationship is cooking, so are the ingredients that make love work. The ingredients are love, understanding, acceptance, trust, forgiveness, appreciation, affection, and mutual respect for each other. When two hearts are dancing in rhythm and both love partners diligently work on the relationship with equal intensity, they create music both hearts can dance to. True love grows from a shared experience. Great sex can be the proof that your relationship is on target. You will feel the body rhythm; you will be in sync. Making love is a dance you learn as you go. Sometimes you lead and sometimes you follow. Two hearts dancing together in the bedroom or wherever they fancy, suggests two lovers in harmony.

Red Hot LoveNote. . . When making love flirts with ecstasy, when you near the blissful satisfaction of a healthy sexual relationship and are both experiencing the ultimate enjoyments of this pleasure zone, you can be sure that your overall relationship is on the right track. Let go! Enjoy each other. Stretch. Take your lovemaking a step further. Innovative couples can find creative ways to embellish their shared intimacies. An oral caress can awaken your taste buds *and* bring xxxtasy to your lover! The tongue is one of the most erotic, excitable, exploratory parts of the human body. A roving tongue will cause major tingles! Using a device instead of the real thing when he cannot perform and she needs sexual release takes the pressure off of him and adds stimulation of another kind to each other. Many glorious adventures await imaginative lovers. Pushing your lovemaking to the limits can make memories that become treasures of the heart. Never settle for anything less than more and better when you make love.

Red Hot LoveNote. . . *For Men Only* ~ Write an occasional "Red Hot LoveNote" to your lover. Here is an example: "Red Hot LoveNote to Sandy . . . When we are making love and we are so close together, I feel so much a part of you. I love the feeling of being inside you. I can feel the rhythm of our song of love; two hearts beating as one. I love you. Larry." Look for sexy things to write about. Things that turn her on. Things that turn each other on. Find the good and exploit it. Tell your lover what pleases you by freely letting her know how good it was for you when she did whatever she did. If you want to turn up the heat try: "Red Hot LoveNote to Sandy . . . I love the way you look up from between my legs when you have me in your mouth. There is an erotic gleam in your eye that tells me you love me and love making love TO me as well as WITH me. Thank you for being so sexually open to explore our fantasies together. I love you. Larry." An erotic Red Hot LoveNote? Perhaps! You can tone it down if you want to. Be bold and be brave. Mean what you say. Write it in such a way that she can feel the love you have for her. When you love each other and really know what turns each other on, share the pleasure you enjoy by leaving a Red Hot LoveNote in a place where she will find it when she is alone.

Red Hot LoveNote. . . Every once in a while, *make plans* to spend several hours making love. That's right! I said "hours." Make it a sexual marathon. Making love for long periods of time can only be accomplished with intention. How can you "last" that long? You will never make the distance if you only have intercourse. Play together. Having fun making love can make it last as long as you both desire. Allow no interruptions. Light some candles. Make mutual pleasure your goal. Take your time. Give each other a full body massage with scented oils without becoming too sexual. Tease. Touch. Taste. Tickle. Hold each other. Whisper "sweet somethings." Don't rush. Express love with words and touch. Mutually stimulate each other with a slow hand. This is called foreplay and for many can be nearly as stimulating as the sexual act itself. When you are both ready . . . really ready, back off. Rest for a while. Be patient. There's no hurry. Let the sexual tension mount. Let orgasm be the bonus, not the goal. Be deliberate. Carefully select the music. Have your love toys nearby. Tell one another how you will pleasure the other. *Men:* Respect the warm-up time required for your lover to be hot enough for easy, smooth penetration, at least 20 to 30 minutes. *Women:* Respect the fact that if rushed, it can be over for a man in about two minutes or less once the fire begins to burn . . . not too fast. For most men, it is difficult to continue once orgasm is experienced. Slow and easy. Resist the urge for penetration too soon. Warm and tender. Take your time. Enjoy each other. Take time out for a cool sip of wine or a sparkling water with a twist of lime. Making love like this takes planning. Put some thought into it. Make love for a while, then taper off and rest for a while. Then begin again. Extend your pleasure of one another. Touch each other the way you know your lover likes to be touched. Put in a few, "That feels good!" or "That's it! A little harder. Oh, yes!" Make a joyful noise. *Women:* Remember, to a man your orgasmic outcry can be an exquisite inspiration. Let yourself go. *Men:* Remember, when you are near orgasm, whispering what is to come can be an incredible catalyst to simultaneous orgasm. Let yourself go. Genuinely seduce each other. Freely express yourself sexually. Put the pleasure of your love partner before your own pleasure. It will be worth it. Experiment with mutually acceptable ways of being connected. You love each other . . . show it! Last as long as you can. Put everything you have into making sure your love partner is satisfied. Make love to her. Make love to him. Make love *with* each other. Let the sexual energy flow freely. Watch love grow! Oh, what fun!

Red Hot LoveNote. . . Arguments call attention to the stuff in our own life that needs to be worked on. It is one of the greatest turnoffs for great sex. Arguing about a problem rarely settles anything. Immature people sometimes start arguments to avoid sex. It is difficult to reach agreement when both love partners are angry and holding on to their position, choosing to be right instead of happy! The resolution of argument should not be victory, but progress. The rules of argument say that one must win and one must lose. This is a bad idea and does little to support a healthy love relationship. You must have agreements about how you communicate about issues and concerns. A few suggested agreements are: stop defending your position and only listen, don't raise your voice (especially watch your TONE of voice), don't argue . . . have a conversation "about" the issues and concerns . . . one that demonstrates respect for your love partner's right to have his or her own opinion about things. Let the other person fully express what is on his or her mind. Take turns doing this. Negotiate a win-win solution, agree to disagree, agree to support each other in keeping your agreements, agree to call attention to the fact that your love partner may be skirting the issues or bringing up "other" stuff to avoid the "real" issue. (Have an agreement about HOW you do this.) If what your partner is saying is causing you anger or resentment, then have agreements about how to talk about that without saying "hurtful" things. There are more agreements, but this will get you started. A calm, low-volume discussion is recommended, the kind that does not seek to make one love partner wrong and the other right. It is a discussion that searches for understanding, one that releases tension and facilitates an emotional break-through that can help your relationship evolve to a new level of love and understanding. It takes TWO to tangle; TWO to have an argument!! No one can "argue" if there is no one to argue with. This is not just your love part-ner's problem. It's yours, too! You both are into being RIGHT or you wouldn't argue. This way of being with each other obviously doesn't work! Don't do this to your relationship! There are three sides to every story – yours, mine and the truth! Wise love partners give up being right in favor of searching for the truth. An argument is NEVER more important than the relationship! It will only cause sex to become an endangered pleasure. If you want great sex . . . reach some new agreements about how to talk about your disagreements.

Red Hot LoveNote. . . Your sexual relationship must entertain your heart and tickle your imagination. Let it be one that causes you to feel aware of the presence of love and glad you are alive to experience it. Lovers who have learned to give, give unselfishly. They give without caring to remember; they do not keep score. Lovers who receive, receive without forgetting. A deep emotional bond is made which has definite physical benefits. Making love must be a shared pleasure for true sexual enjoyment to occur. The reward for sharing in the experience is countless, uninhibited sexual adventures together; close encounters of the angelic kind. Remember, foreplay IS an aphrodisiac. Imagination enhances arousal and great sex is fueled by the heat of your imagination.

Red Hot LoveNote. . . *For Women Only* ~ In a survey of 1000 men conducted by *Glamour* magazine, when asked, "How would you feel if a partner masturbated in front of you?," 56% said they would be "turned on," 26% said they would be fascinated – "I might learn something," 11% said they would be turned off and 7% said they would be hurt, i.e., "Aren't I enough?" Taking care of yourself is the most personal thing you can do with yourself. If you have a secure, healthy and committed relationship and are looking for sexual adventure, imagine the thrill you might feel if you could allow your lover to watch while you turn yourself on. Imagine the freedom of sexual expression you may experience if you could share your secret pleasure with him. Be brave. If you confess your secret, would it turn him on? Off? In a lovemaking interlude, lying quietly together, begin to gently touch yourself as only you can. Break the rules. Smile. Say nothing. Let *him* discover your busy hands. Make love to yourself. When he notices, don't stop. With one hand begin softly stroking his penis. Feel the emotions and desire swell. (Pun intended). In the heat of passion, turning yourself on and allowing your lover to notice is very exciting. Just do it. There is something to be said about taking the first step while you are still afraid. Talk about overcoming sexual inhibitions! Do you dare? He may be in the 56%!

Red Hot LoveNote. . . It's fun to share your fantasies with your lover. You must have agreements. The agreement is to know that you are only "talking about" your secret fantasy and are not saying you MUST do it. Be careful with this one. Speaking fantasy can be dangerous if the trust level is low in your relationship. Two lovers who really love each other, who totally trust each other, can discuss virtually any imaginable fantasy without fear that their lover will pressure them to participate in it or become jealous by the mention of it. Forbidden are things that would cause any serious damage to the relationship if they were actually acted out. Pretending together is safe and healthy when your relationship is both secure and solid. This kind of oral foreplay can light the spark that can produce wild passion beyond that which either of you have experienced.

Red Hot LoveNote. . . Reaching satisfaction with your sex life only and always has to do with your attitude about your overall relationship. What you think about and speak about, you bring about! If you talk with others about your relationship in terms of disappointment, anger and resentment rather than in terms of endearment, you are setting you, your partner and your relationship up for a fall. You are the solitary power and driving force behind your attitude. Only you have the power to change it. This is not rocket science! If your attitude about your relationship is one of blame, perhaps you need to look into the mirror to see who is responsible for that attitude. "What about my *needs?*" If your needs are not being met, make some new requests. That is your responsibility, not your partner's. To continue to hold on to an attitude about your relationship that doesn't take you where you want to go is destructive. If changes are needed . . . make them!

Red Hot LoveNote. . . *For Men Only* ~ To raise the level of sexual intensity, whisper words that are likely to cause your lover to become hot, wet and eager to make love. It's okay to talk while making love. You can arouse passion with words. Paint a hot, steamy picture of what you will do to help her more playfully and passionately enjoy the moment. Learn to make love with your voice. Tantalize. Be descriptive. Don't hold back. "I love to make love with you." Softly massage her breasts. "Your nipples are getting hard. I love the way your breast fills my hand." Circle her nipples with your fingers. "That feels good, doesn't it?" Got the picture? If you know your lover well, you know how far you can go. Words, softly spoken, can tweak her hot buttons – even without touch. They can raise the arousal level to a point where there will no longer be a need for words, only the quiet colliding of two hot bodies exploding in orgasm together.

Red Hot LoveNote. . . When you place a high value on your sexual relationship, you will find more pleasure in it. When you are both energetic in your pursuit of it, bells ring! Be intentional about striving for ways to improve it. When you can freely express with words what making love with your love partner is like, how it feels, and what you would like to try next time, then you can explore together the erotic treats that God has given you the choice to create. You must learn to continue doing those things that you do together that keeps your love alive. Anything of value must be managed to stay in existence.

Red Hot LoveNote. . . When it comes to great sex, past performance is no guarantee of future results. Sound familiar? This caveat is as relevant to relationships as it is to financial investments. How exciting you were in bed last week was only a reflection of the condition of the relationship at that point in time. The intensity of your bedroom antics likely reflects the overall condition of the relationship moment to moment. The degree to which you focus your energy upon doing the little things that demonstrate your love and support for your relationship is the degree to which you can count on the erotic side of your relationship to prosper. It's an investment in your relationship that points you in the right direction; it puts you both on the path to pleasure and bliss.

Red Hot LoveNote. . . There is great power in words. "Oh, yes! Touch me there!" "I love it when you put your tongue in that spot." Saying words that signal your ecstasy is a turn-on for most love partners. We often assume that our lover knows that he or she is pleasing us. Never assume anything. Your lover cannot read your mind. If you want the person to do something . . . say so. If you want your lover to stop doing something . . . say so. When you have the courage to say what's real for you in the moment, you will find your lovemaking getting better by the minute. Words encourage. Even a brief whimper is better than nothing. Gently guide the person's hand to where it feels good. Let your love partner know he or she is doing something that gives pleasures to you. Exert sexual word power!

Red Hot LoveNote. . . *For Men Only* ~ Be generous with your kisses! Remember to *always* give her a good night kiss. Giving her a kiss on the back of her shoulder when she thought you were asleep will bring a smile to her face you can almost see in the darkness. Even a hurried peck on the cheek will not go unnoticed. A smile, a wink and a kiss can speak louder than words. Stop what you are doing and greet her with a kiss when you arrive home before she does. Blow her an unexpected kiss from across the dining room table. Leave a note with only kisses (xxxxxxx's) on her dressing room mirror or computer screen. Sign it, "Guess who loves you?" Give her hand three squeezes to say "I love you" and kiss her on the cheek somewhere in public. A lingering kiss in the driveway as you leave for the office is always nice. Let the neighbors watch! Give her a juicy kiss that makes some noise! Sneak up behind her and kiss her gently on the neck, say nothing and quietly disappear. After a romantic evening together, a kiss in the moonlight will make the night complete. When she is sad, comfort her and with noticeable sensitivity, kiss the tears away. Kisses help moments of sorrow fade into the distance. Shower her with kisses when you make love. Kiss her everywhere. Dare to give her the forbidden kiss. During your passionate encounters, make your kisses part of the main event.

Red Hot LoveNote. . . The passion of your relationship and your commitment to it will express itself in all other areas of your life, with family, friends and business associates. It spills over into everything you do. Every joy shared brings more love and loving. The enthusiasm you have for loving one another shines for the whole world to see. The love, irrepressible desire and passion you share have their way of expressing generously back into the relationship and to all those around you. Happiness is catching. Partners who are committed to spreading the joy of a healthy relationship will be more intentionally inclined and confidently dedicated to continue to work together. An additional reward is experiencing the erotic pleasures that become available in the sanctuary of the boudoir.

Red Hot LoveNote. . . Sexual romance is invented. It won't come to you and your lover unless you decide that what you both want is a satisfying sexual relationship, full of adventure and sexual romance. It is possible. It is not something that you have to wait for. You can create it yourself and you can begin now. You must invent *a fictitious tale of wonderful and extraordinary events characterized by much imagination and idealization* and both be bold and willing to live the sexual part of your relationship that way. By the way, the words in italics are what Webster has to say about romance. When you live your life that way – full out – extraordinary sexual events are possible. Be willing to explore new sexual arenas in which to play. Be romantic. Be a sexual romantic. Become a pyromantic. Light the fire! Imagination turns up the heat. Being romantic is great. Being romantic doesn't always have to lead to sex. However, being sexually romantic is a mutually invented way of being that is sure to pave the way to greater sexual satisfaction. It helps give meaning to making love. It helps you understand that making love is more than just sex or a quick tumble in the hay. It's making love! You can feel the love. You can touch it, hear it, smell it, taste it. You can watch it in action. Never worry about getting it right. Let go of "how" it should happen or "how" it should feel. Let it happen naturally. It will happen the way it does and it will feel the way it feels. The only rule is to do what mutually feels good and is sexually satisfying. You get there by being sexually romantic. It's speaking romantically in a sexual way . . . in a palatable way. No crudeness allowed. It's being romantic with a sexual twist. It's not some way that someone can tell you how to be. You invent it together, in your very own special way.

Red Hot LoveNote. . . *For Women Only* ~ Write an occasional "Red Hot LoveNote" to your lover. Here is a lukewarm example: "Red Hot LoveNote to Larry . . . I love the way you honor my wishes when I only want to cuddle. Your gentle touch means so much to me; your arms around me; our legs folded together on crumpled sheets . . . a perfect fit. I could feel your body telling me that you wanted me. Next time I promise to make love TO you! Sandy." If you want your love partner to become more intentional about *being* a great lover, tell him how it feels when you are together. Be specific. Light his fire. Take a match and slightly burn the edges of the note and slip it into his briefcase or attach it to the rearview mirror of his car. If you want to turn up the heat: "Red Hot LoveNote to Larry . . . I love the soft, moist touch of your lips on my breasts and the way you gently massage my nipples with your tongue. What a turn-on! I love being your "breast" friend. AND . . . when you kiss me where you know it feels good, it takes my breath away! Sometime I'll show you how I touch myself. Thanks for being such a great lover! Sandy." Say what matters to you. Use words that titillate his imagination. Feel free to offer suggestions you may ordinarily be too inhibited to say aloud. Wouldn't it be a wonderful surprise if your partner were interested in the same initiatives?

Red Hot LoveNote. . . The partner who does not DO more to make the relationship work is not committed to the relationship. The sad truth is, you can tell the relationship is over when one love partner REFUSES to work on the relationship. Relationships require work. However, you must do what you can to avoid a struggle. When relationships become a struggle, you can be sure one partner is not pulling his or her fair share of the load. One cannot do the work of two. This often causes you to feel as if love were leaving you alone again. Committed lovers continually reinvest themselves in their relationship. They know if they don't let IT down, it will never let them down. They don't just try, they do! They can count on their love partner's love and support during those times when they would almost rather quit than let the other partner be right again. It takes no strength to let go . . . only courage. They remember previous successes as a source of confidence to help them move through struggles when they occur. They have a devotion to learning new skills and are forever committed to put them into practice. Commitment challenges your perspective. When commitment is present, you feel loved; you continue to work together. When it is real love, it will not leave you alone!

Red Hot LoveNote. . . We cannot move past our feelings to something better unless we first experience, then express those feelings! This is true for all feelings. They must be acknowledged and felt. Feelings of anger and disappointment must be experienced to get past them to the good stuff. Feelings of warmth, love, understanding, sexual excitement, and all of those wonderful, warm, fuzzy feelings must also be experienced and expressed to reach a higher level of understanding about the spiritual connectedness that occurs when we make love with our partner. Sexual feelings are aroused to be expressed. They must be expressed to be experienced. Be sexually expressive. It really is okay. The more we express to our partner how we think great sex *should* feel, the more freedom we will have to experience the greatness of our next sexual moment together.

Red Hot LoveNote. . . *For Men Only* ~ Women can often tell a man's interest in them by the length of his attention span. It's one thing to pay attention and quite another to continue to pay attention until she has had her say. Make sure your eyes are on her! Give her as much time as she needs to say what is in her heart. Totally focus on what she is saying and stay quiet. She wants your attention. She needs to know you are really hearing what she is saying. Don't try to fix anything . . . only listen, then (choosing your words very carefully) acknowledge that she has been heard.

Red Hot LoveNote. . . Never, never talk about what isn't going right with your lovemaking while you are making love. Pressure is the enemy of pleasure. To talk about your love partner's lack of interest, impotence, lack of enthusiasm or that he should do this or that she should do that, while you are in the throes of passion is never acceptable! If it is soft and you want it to stay that way, point it out! Talking about it is one sure way to kiss it good night! It can put undue pressure on your love partner that could cause a total withholding of future affection in the bedroom. There is a time and place for everything. While you are making love is neither the time nor the place. In this scenario, it is never a good idea to talk about your partner's shortcomings. (Pun intended!) However, if your lover is doing something you find offensive or unacceptable, that is the exception. Tell your mate to stop or simply use your hands to stop or slow down the action.

Red Hot LoveNote... Not one of the old myths about the harmful effects of masturbation is true. It does not matter how much you do it. However, the exception may be that masturbating too frequently can diminish the desire for sex, especially if you and your partner have relationship issues that need resolution. Masturbation puts you more in touch with your body when you experiment with your own sexual responsiveness. Here is the value of masturbation. Once you discover how to give yourself pleasure it is easier to show and tell your love partner what makes you feel good. You take nothing from your relationship when you self-stimulate. When you get married, some believe that you should leave masturbation at the threshold now that you have a partner. Not so. Masturbation can be a great substitute for intercourse when you have no partner, or when your love partner is not in the mood or unavailable. It will not make your marriage partner obsolete. Reaching orgasm by self-stimulation feels good. Overcoming the guilt that may have been instilled as a child, however, is often difficult. The majority of men and women practice solo sex and some suffer the same irrational guilt. There is no shame in taking care of yourself. Sometimes it feels good just to be able to satisfy your own sexual needs in your own way without having to consider anyone else.

Red Hot LoveNote. . . *For Women Only* ~ Men need more than a lover who will lie motionless on the bed with her arms out to her sides. Put some action in your lovemaking – a wiggle here, a wiggle there. Be alive. Move around. A man needs to know you are more than willing. Touch him. Bathe him with your kisses. Make love to HIM. If you don't know what he likes . . . ask him or take the initiative and see if you can really turn him on!

Red Hot LoveNote. . . If it tastes delicious, eat it! There is more than one reason to introduce flavors into your lovemaking. For some people sex doesn't taste so good. Bodily fluids mostly have a distinctive salty tang that appeals to some and not to others. Being pleasured by your partner orally feels good, but if your lover finds the taste challenging, you may want to try pleasing his or her tongue first. Honey, jelly, spreadable chocolate, bubbly wine, edible love oils and gels all taste good. I call them gourmet appeteazers. They make oral sex tasty. Chocolate kisses. Ummmm, good! Things could get a little messy, so be prepared. Stay away from acidic, alkaline, abrasive substances, very spicy items or anything too hot or too cold. If it irritates your tongue, it will distract from the intended pleasure and could be harmful. Visit an adult store together and check out the many products offered that can increase the excitement and the possibility for tasteful oral sex.

Red Hot LoveNote. . . *For Men Only* ~ Write your sweetie an erotic love letter. There is a little voyeurism in all of us. Every man has, at one time or another, watched as his lover slipped behind a towel after coming from a slow, sensual shower or caught a glimpse of her body as she slipped into something more comfortable. Describe this scenario. Write about how seeing her like that stimulates your desire to make love with her. Describe the way you feel while watching her walk along the beach picking up seashells, or the way her body moves while making love. She will be excited that you noticed. This letter could become her talisman of passion. Put some thought into it. Visit a local greeting card store and peruse the romantic cards for some ideas. Tell her how it will be the next time you make love. Be specific. Don't be bashful. You may want to tell her how special it is for you to gently touch her breasts or rub her neck or whatever makes you both feel good when you are together. Have your intention be to have your lover understand the warmth, romance, passion and love behind the words.

Red Hot LoveNote. . . It's never a good time to discuss sexual problems in the bedroom. Reserve these conversations for some other place. A cool glass of wine and some warm conversation around the table on the patio or anywhere except the bedroom is better. Keep the bedroom pristine! Think of the bedroom as your pleasure palace, a place where sexual energy is expressed and where you can rest and rejuvenate for whatever is ahead. You will not want to have memories of what *was* in a place reserved for what *is*.

Red Hot LoveNote. . .Being intimate is not just making love. Touching, being together, only cuddling, having steamy conversation, walking together in the park, talking about things that matter, holding hands, and kissing are a few ways to experience intimacy. Great sex is the result of diligent effort by love partners who are committed to experiencing intimacy in ALL of its many forms. Making love is the ultimate shared intimacy.

Red Hot LoveNote. . . *For Men Only* ~ You begin making love to your partner when you give her a smile, tell her she looks and smells good and by declaring a cheery, "Good morning!" It continues when you take a moment from your work at the office and give her a brief phone call, one that says, "I was thinking about you!" Perhaps we could call this *all-day foreplay!* If you always expect this variety of kindness to lead to sex, you are missing the point. Being there for her when she needs a shoulder to lean on and being a committed listener, one who offers her your complete attention when she only wants to talk, is all part of being a good love partner. Paying sincere compliments, equally sharing household responsibilities and being her best friend is not just being good to her to get what you want! It expresses love. Women can detect insincerity a mile away. When you offer her your complete attention, you give her a wonderful gift. You call attention to the fact that you respect her as a woman *and* your friend without demanding anything in return.

Red Hot LoveNote. . . When you are angry, rarely is the first thought on your mind: "I can hardly wait until things get back to 'no anger,' so we can make passionate love!" Can you imagine how great things might be if that *were* your first thought? That way of thinking certainly will get you through the situation more quickly. Great sex is but one of the rewards for intimacy. Rarely are you further apart than when anger rears its ugly head. Most people find it difficult to express love when they are angry. When things happen that you choose to be angry about, you can choose to work through the anger and be rewarded with the kind of intimacy that can only make room for great sex. Work through anger with finesse. Do it with delicate skill. Stretch. Be someone different this time. See how that feels. Listen. Don't react. Listen, then respond with understanding. Often we become so defensive, while our love partner is venting, we begin to think about how we are going to justify our own position and forget to listen. This way of being keeps you in the danger zone. You are angry because something happened and you chose to feel that way. You stay there because you don't know what to do or if you do, you may be afraid that doing it will make you look weak. Taking a bold step forward is the salvation of your relationship. The next time you have a serious conversation and anger shows up, demonstrate your love; keep your mouth shut and listen to your love partner's story. Take that first step and acknowledge the other person's feelings with sincerity, the first step back to intimacy. Intimacy then creates its own reward.

Red Hot LoveNote. . . It's okay to just *snuggle!* Make plans to spend some time just holding each other. No sex. Just a warm, tender embrace. You can feel the love.

Red Hot LoveNote. . . To avoid boredom in the bedroom you must have variety in the relationship. Having sex the same way every time can cause your lovemaking to become stale and commonplace. Make love in the guest room. Shower or bathe together. Hump in the hot tub. Get out your bag of love toys. Take turns initiating sex. Indoors? Outdoors? Make love in the back seat of your car in the garage. Try different positions. Do it with the lights on! Spend an evening at the "No-Tell" Motel. Ready yourselves by watching a sexy video together. Choose different music. Have fun fooling around near the flickering flames of your fireplace. Make love in the morning before you take off for the office. Turn off ALL the lights and discover the power of touch. Use your imagination. Take a drive and park! Spend some time together writing down interesting places you might like to make love, then exchange lists. Send your partner a suggestive note with a new location. Be spontaneous! Go where there is no path . . . and leave a trail! Put this book down RIGHT NOW, find your partner and make love!

Red Hot LoveNote. . . *For Men Only* ~ Having problems with premature ejaculation? Learn to be aware of your point of ejaculatory inevitability, that moment when you know if you keep pumping you will not be able to hold back, that you can't stop from coming. Learn to control your timing. If your penis has a hair-trigger this can be remedied; however, you may need to practice by masturbating to learn where that point of control is. Light your own fire, but don't blow on the flame! Find that moment of ejaculatory inevitability and learn to stop before you reach it. Exercising self-control demonstrates respect for your love partner. If you want to extend the time of those magic moments with your lover, try this. While making love, if you feel yourself about to go over the edge, put your thumb on the top of the ridge of your penis and your two fingers on the bottom and lightly squeeze the corona of your penis to help you hold back. Rest for a few minutes. Cuddle, kiss and fondle for awhile, then continue. If you take the time to bring her to orgasm before you enter her, it really doesn't matter how long you last.

Red Hot LoveNote. . . A "quickie," anyone? There is nothing wrong with a brief sexual encounter. Sometimes you just wanna have pure unadulterated sex and then get on with whatever you were doing. At one time or another, most of us think about it, but seldom request it. Quickies are great too! They are a quick turn-on – admittedly, sometimes not too romantic – but all part of incredible sex. They satisfy a healthy urge to connect with the one you love, to express love briefly and so to sleep or whatever is next. Be spontaneous! Quickies can serve as a healthy way to relieve the stress of the day in a carefree, yet loving way, AND there must be agreements. If you can BOTH agree to an occasional quickie, do it; if not . . . don't! How about doing it in the back seat of your car, on the edge of the hot tub, on the floor in the bathroom, in the back yard under a tree on a blanket or on the kitchen table? Quickies can be useful for a quick connection to satisfy your lover even when you may not be in the mood. This applies to both women and men. Most men would love for their lover to suggest some fast action. Almost anyone can be turned on long enough for a quickie when they know they are not expected to perform long and hard. Quickies keep the fire of love alive. Acknowledge your desire for a quickie to your love partner and watch what happens. Enjoy!

Red Hot LoveNote. . . Smart love partners take some time to bathe before they make love. Take a long hot shower or a leisurely warm bath. Clean lovers are always ready for any erotic surprises their lover may be willing to undertake.

Red Hot LoveNote. . . *For Women Only* ~ Let's face it. As men become older, their testosterone level drops. Some lose interest in sex. Others become afraid of getting older and a few become impotent or experience sporadic periods of impotency. For some men, it takes longer to have an erection, there may be less ejaculate, and it takes longer between erections, but they can still have great sex until the day they die! Unless there is a diagnosed medical problem, it may be only in his mind. How should a woman react when a man becomes impotent during sex? First, understand that it isn't about you! It can happen to the best of men. Learn to love it flaccid. There are a lot of pleasurable things you can do with a limp penis. If he is unable or is concerned or under stress, you must take over if you want to continue to have fun. Good hand and mouth work will almost always assure a return engagement as a reward for your efforts. Titillate your lover with gentle, slow strokes, remembering to use enough pressure and making use of the total skin surface. Use your imagination.

Red Hot LoveNote. . . Partners who manifest a lack of sexual confidence, an inability to truly let go sexually, who have an obsession with sexual privacy, or guilt associated with masturbation or who are guarded in speaking freely about sex can alienate themselves from their own bodies and from their love partner. Expressing sexuality is not sinful, disgusting or evil. Making love can be a pleasurable way of entering a higher state of consciousness, increasing spiritual awareness, and it is a powerful act of emotional and physical bonding. Being loved and making love are basic human needs. Taking all the pleasure you want and need on the way to orgasm is an erotic ritual, one worthy of praise and adoration. Lovers with partners who need sexual healing must exercise patience, understanding and love. Moving from guilt to being sexually free does not happen overnight. Gentle persuasion and a nurturing kind of encouragement contribute to fulfilling our need for this energetic connection and the pleasure that attends it. We all have loving, pleasure-receptive bodies. Learning ways to satisfy our needs – free of guilt – can be cause for us to be grounded, calm, full of joy and relaxed enough to let go and to be at peace with ourselves within so we can express our eroticism with our partner outwardly, freely and in loving ways.

Red Hot LoveNote. . . When your lover touches or kisses you in a special way, that is always a good time to say how it feels. It is important to verbally express yourself; say so out loud when you know you will be heard and understood.

Red Hot LoveNote. . . As your relationship matures, the love you share grows deeper. You can more easily accept what you have together and go with it! True devotion to your forever love partner becomes the bias. Sex becomes more pleasurable because it expresses a couple's mutual adoration for one another. It is not just an erotic high, it is a very special form of communicating your love for each other. It is nurtured by acceptance, respect, generosity, spontaneity, and romance. Amorous feelings thrive on renewed stimulation. Your willingness to help each other achieve orgasm creates those very special moments worth remembering. It is your relationship that makes sex special, not the other way around. Blend making love with compassion and tenderness. Accepting the whole body as a source of pleasure, choosing the right time, place and being willing to expend the energy to feel and experience orgasm are needs that must be met. Having a full orgasm with the one you love is evidence of the trust you have for each other.

Red Hot LoveNote. . . *For Men Only* ~ Introducing a bag of love toys to your lovemaking session can help you get your partner ready for the big "O" and relieve you of the pressure of having to do all the work with your penis. Women need more time and the right kind of stimulation to be ready for orgasm. Her climactic reflex is triggered by a buildup of erotic stimulation brought on by one of or a combination of the following: romantic thoughts, self-stimulation, partner-assisted masturbation, oral sex, intermittent intercourse and love toys. The arousal level must last long enough to push her near or over the edge. Love toys can embellish the buildup time. A vibrator can provide desirable motion and stimulate in a way that the penis cannot. After you have an orgasm, it's pretty much curtains for your penis. A woman's sexual energy can extend far beyond your own capabilities. If she wants to continue, a vibrator can come in handy. A fully rested, responsive woman when sexually aroused can extend a single orgasm to multiple orgasms when you continue to titillate her most sexually sensitive zone. It is quite possible that during her extended arousal you may again be turned on and be ready to go again. Love toys can maximize her pleasure wave when you are too exhausted to continue. Have extra batteries on the nightstand!

Red Hot LoveNote. . . Sexy assignment: Recall a night when the two of you passionately made love, the one where you were – on purpose, so impetuous, torrid, daring, and lusty that it became one of those nights you both call "memorable bliss." You both were in heat! "Is it hot in here, or is it US?" It was a night where the sex was so good that even the neighbors had a cigarette. Do *that* again! If you have trouble remembering, you are past due. Working together, you can both turn a spark into a flame. Get busy!

Red Hot LoveNote. . . If sex shows up as boring, you have only to look into the mirror to see the problem. The admission of boredom suggests that you are saying to your lover, "Make me happy! Excite ME!" It is never only up to your partner to do all the work. Expecting to receive your happiness and sexual satisfaction from your partner alone is not taking responsibility for your part of the sexual relationship and can only lead to continued disappointment. That's boring. You must give to receive; be exciting to experience excitement. Cease being so predicable. For things to change for the better, you must make a conscious effort to do YOUR part to eliminate the boredom by understanding where the boredom originates. What you are currently saying, thinking and doing for the relationship you have with yourself either moves you closer to the one you love or further away. Remember to include yourself among those you love and watch the boredom, monotony, apathy and dreariness in the bedroom disappear. Love changes everything.

Red Hot LoveNote. . . Feeling especially adventurous? Visit an adult store to select a few love toys! Often intense stimulation of another kind can be experienced by using a battery operated vibrator, or various other instruments of pleasure. You may be delightfully surprised at the numerous and creative ways people have invented to add spice and variety to your sexual encounters. Having the courage to visit the local sex shop TOGETHER is a good way to begin to be rid of any sexual inhibitions either of you may have. Notice I said together. This venture can be an adventure when it is mutually agreeable and when it becomes something you can do together to increase the excitement level of your relationship.

Red Hot LoveNote. . . *For Men Only* ~ Learn to enjoy the "afterglow" or "afterplay" with your partner. After your lover has had an orgasm or is signaling you to slow down . . . ease off but don't leave her alone just yet. Talk to her, gently stroke her body, softly caress her breasts, let your fingers do their dance in that slippery place where you know it feels good. Keep making love to her quietly, slowing until she's come all the way down. Let her ride the "wave." Be gentle. A man can have an orgasm and go to sleep with no sense of loss. *Your behavior after sex is a window to your true feelings about her.* By nature, she will require much more sensitivity from you in those first few moments after sex. Take as much time as she needs. Your postcoital posture, simply lying together, hugging and holding in the fading passion, makes her feel protected. It is a luxury you must afford her. It is how she measures the man. She will appreciate you for it.

Red Hot LoveNote. . . If your sex life is stagnant, perhaps it's time to do something different. Remember, if you always do what you've always done, you will always get what you have always gotten. There is nothing wrong with planning to make love. Anticipation can even make it better. At least once a week, plan some sensual time together. Schedule intimacy. Movement is the cure for sexual stagnation. Moving to new things, to new heights, to new agreements and exploring the desires you both have can renew enthusiasm for making love, for embarking on an exciting sexual adventure together. Use your imagination! What do you want? Express it to your love partner.

Red Hot LoveNote. . . A commitment to self is not being selfish. It does not preclude having a commitment to your relationship. Having a healthy love relationship full of love and great sex always begins with having a healthy relationship with yourself. Only two whole, healthy people can design that kind of partnership together. For you to be able to nurture and fully support your relationship together, you must be committed to always take care of yourself first! Your partner must come second. It is important to understand that each individual is only and always responsible for taking care of his or her self. Your partner cannot do this for you. To experience the joy of your relationship to its fullest, you must be strong, self-confident, alert, self-assured, healthy, energetic, spirited, vibrant, decisive, expressive, happy, independent, and passionate – all qualities that each person can only generate within himself or herself. Two broken people cannot fix each other. Both partners must take complete responsibility for their own personal growth and development. Each must have an intention to continually encourage and support their partner in this process. Being responsible begins with the willingness to understand that you are the creator of who you are, the kind of relationship you have and what you do. It is a grace you give to yourself.

Red Hot LoveNote. . . If you always do what you've always done, you will always get what you have always gotten! How boring! Variety is the spice of an extraordinary sexual relationship! Embark on a quest for mutually agreeable sexual thrills and you may discover a new way of relating to each other. The mind goes where it is most stimulated. Your most sensual sex organ is your mind, your very own imagination. Utilize it to its fullest. Break some new ground. Mutually agreeable experimentation is sexually stimulating. Create new sexual possibilities for each other. Don't just do it. Talk about it. Agreement is important here. Where there is no agreement, there could be disaster. Have a stimulating, open conversation about something you would like to try that is different. The conversation itself is foreplay. It's exciting to watch your lover be turned on by only words.

Red Hot LoveNote. . . *For Women Only* ~ Someone once said if you know how to type, roller skate, or use an ATM, you can learn how to have an orgasm. Begin with self-stimulation. If you are able to reach orgasm that way, you can reach orgasm when you are with your lover. While making love, purposefully fine-tune your masturbation technique, what you do with your fingers, your body, and your mind – while you are with him. Rather than assume his penis alone will do the trick, touch yourself while you are having intercourse. Make yourself feel good. Don't be shy. A very small percentage of women are able to achieve orgasm through coital stimulation alone. Include your lover in this endeavor. Most likely, when he notices, it will be a tantalizing turn-on. Embellish your orgasm technique for him. Determining on your own, then showing him how your body responds to your own touch is imperative. That comes first. Of course, your love partner needs to do his part, too. Whisper how much you enjoy helping him make you come in words he can understand and he will lavish your body with all the pleasure you so richly deserve.

Red Hot LoveNote. . . When the emotions of petty differences give way to anger, resentment and nearly irreconcilable differences, it puts sex on the endangered pleasures list. Those generous and compassionate spirits who choose to let go of being right in favor of happiness will have many more memorable opportunities to celebrate love.

Red Hot LoveNote. . . Making love is an energy exchange, the energy of love, promise and commitment. Making love is not something you approach with cautious enthusiasm. Lovers who surrender to each other experience intense emotional excitement – allowing the promise of love to fulfill itself – when they connect with vital enthusiasm. This kind of energy is not always vigorous, rigorous or wild. It is often full of life, playful, quietly erotic and passively stimulating. This kind of fervent coupling is the reward for always doing the best you can in all areas of your relationship, not just in the bedroom. How much your partner contributes to this exchange of sexual energy reflects that person's love and commitment to you and the relationship.

Red Hot LoveNote. . . *For Men Only* ~ It's time that men exhibit respect for a woman's whole body. Your love partner is not just a receptacle. She is a warm, passionate woman with feelings. She has breasts, hands, fingers, legs, buttocks, ear lobes, feet, and various other parts of her body that deserve love also. A woman often responds more easily when you talk to her while you are making love. Describe the softness of her breasts; the tautness of her nipples; the satiny feel of her hair. Rub the bottoms of her feet while asking her to tell you if it feels good. One of her greatest assets is her natural perfume. Let her know you relish the scent of her skin, hair, breasts, genitals, the whole woman. There is no other like her. Make love to the whole woman.

Red Hot LoveNote. . . A heart full of love has no shadows of the past, no past to run from, only a present to enjoy and a future to step into. Seek opportunities to create great memories together. Create some sexual moments you can forever embrace. You know, the ones where you get that tingling feeling whenever you stop and think about them. Move forward. Don't look back. Delight in exploration. Be unafraid. In the absence of fear, love makes all things possible. This is no ordinary love.

Red Hot LoveNote. . . Love is the supreme emotion. We feel it when someone we love expresses their love for us in a very special way. Real love is indescribable. Paramahansa Yogananda once said, "To define Love is very difficult, for the same reason that words cannot fully describe the flavor of an orange. You have to taste the fruit to know its flavor. So with Love!" Making love with one another – notice, I said "with," not to – is the ultimate way of expressing love in a way that heats up the relationship in a Divine and glorious way. It is a very personal and empowering experience. Never become guilty of withholding the effort necessary for love to make itself known to your partner through the mutual exchange of sexual energy. Some people withhold effort. For your relationship to become rich with undying love and fantastic sex, you must treat your partner with respect and dignity. The emotional honesty that comes from putting forth the sincere effort to express love leads to genuine intimacy and understanding. The willingness to take this action is proof of your belief in the love of the relationship.

Red Hot LoveNote. . . *For Women Only* ~ Every man needs to have a supporting love partner who will not overwhelm him with her feelings every time HE does begin to let her know how HE feels. From a man's perspective, some women can talk a situation into the ground. Men don't do it that way! Men like to get to the point, without interruptions, focusing on the solution as soon as the problem is learned, most often never communicating why they aren't talking and sharing with their partner. His silent successes, if any, contribute to the relationship and need to be shared. When you listen, he learns it is safe to say what is in his heart – without judgments – and he is more likely to allow himself to become vulnerable again. Women don't do it that way! Often without knowing it, they alienate men by shower-ing them with how THEY feel in the same conversation. Perhaps only listening might work better. You want that from him. Offer him the same courtesy. You will have plenty of time to let him know how you feel at another time. Listening validates his feelings. It helps overcome his fear of being vulnerable. Some men don't feel like they are very good at communicating with their partner. Have your fore-play with him be encouraging him to talk and promise only to listen. You can demonstrate your love and understand-ing by offering him a safe place to speak his feelings.

Red Hot LoveNote. . . Give up any consistent routine you may have while making love. Vary the process. Make love like you drive when you are in heavy traffic. You slow down, then you speed up, then you slow down, then you speed up. You may even choose rest stops to refresh the mind and rejuvenate the body. An assortment of positions and places to have great sex plus a collection of play toys and stimulating dialogue add to the medley of exciting ideas from which lovers can choose pleasure. The sexual side of relationships must be studied and enacted to be perfected. Touch, kiss, handle, lick, stroke, nuzzle, play, snuggle, pet, tongue, hold, nestle, fondle, squeeze, fool around, hug, compliment, notice, frolic, amuse, embrace, caress, yield with abandon, and totally surrender. Raise the bar! Say "yes" to each other. There are a lot of ways to make sex great and only a few ways to make it bad.

Red Hot LoveNote. . . Magic happens! It happens when you trust your lover enough to let go and experience whatever is happening in the moment. When you are making love, a lot of sexual energy is generated. Focus on the feelings you are feeling instead of what you *think* you should feel or *how* you should feel. Remember, you are responsible for your own feelings and your own pleasure. The more you put into it, the more you get from the experience. Enjoy and relish the moment. Let go of your expectations and enjoy the magic of being sexually *active* with one another.

Red Hot LoveNote. . . *For Men Only* ~ Is it true that bigger is better? Not necessarily. Most women don't care. It's not the size of the wand, it's how you perform the magic! Size is not as important as learning the skills necessary to make her know that you are more interested in expressing love than just getting your rocks off. Making love is not only about intercourse. Only about a third of women have orgasm by penetration, regardless of size. It's easier to help your love partner reach new heights of pleasure by whispering words of love, gently caressing her with your roaming hands and rushing fingers, and showering her body with kisses, to say nothing of allowing all the time she needs to be ready for the finale. Excluding medical difficulties, almost every woman can have an orgasm if she wants to, is able to trust you enough to totally relax and receives the appropriate amount of *uninterrupted* stimulation. An erotic way to help her reach orgasm is to place HER fingers on her clitoris and let her know it is okay for her to touch herself there while you are inside her. Or allow her to be an active participant with a vibrator and watch the excitement level soar. It is more important to learn about making a woman feel good than to be concerned about the size of your penis. "It's not the size of the ship that matters but how long it takes the seamen to disembark."

Red Hot LoveNote. . . Desire is in every lover's heart. If you do not feel it, it may be that you have both allowed the sexual music you once made together to gradually fade away! No music. No dance. No dance . . . no desire FOR the dance. Always consider the consequences of neglect. When you do not serve your partner's sexual needs, desire withers away. It puts passion on hold. Making music together feeds energy to the dancers. While it is true that often with time, sexual desire may wane, it is not true that it has to stay that way. Desire always comes after thought. The mind is the primary source of sexual arousal. You do not have to FEEL desire to make love. Remembering the magic of past moments together attends to this process. Not letting go of whatever is keeping you from expressing love for your partner because you lack desire is depriving the relationship of one of its most important aspects. Desire often reappears while doing what brings you and your partner pleasure. That's where that magical dance of the hearts begins – in the doing of it. When the music of one heart becomes the shared music of two hearts, you will find two hearts dancing together in a communion of provocative sexual rhythm. What a sight to behold! We think it's the music that stirs our soul. It is those silent thoughts that come from the heart, the ones that once again bring forth desire. Desire is in every lover's heart.

Red Hot LoveNote. . . *For Women Only* ~ Take your lover on an adventurous ride to nowhere. (Only you know for sure!) You need to plan ahead. As far as he knows, there is no planned destination. Let him know you need to have some quiet time with him . . . alone. Chill a pair of wine glasses and a bottle of his favorite wine in a cooler. Dress sexy. Wear a loose fitting dress with no panties or bra. Be brazen. Touch him. Put your hand near his crotch to give him a hint as to why you wanted to get him out of the house . . . and alone. Tease. Blow him kisses. Flirt. Run your fingers through his hair. Initiate sex! Drive to a quiet, secluded spot, pull over, get in the back seat and make love.

Red Hot LoveNote. . . Cherish the idea of remembering those special moments you shared together in the beginning, the ones that brought you together in the first place. Sit down together some quiet evening and make some notes. In the right setting and in the right mood, you will both be able to recreate some of those romantic moments that are worthy of reflection. Exchange notes. Talk about what you both would be willing to do to again fan the sexual flame. Dream up some new scenarios and share them with each other. It will help you reconnect and open up the lines of communication. Intimate conversations about your sexual relationship is a prerequisite to having great sex. Share and explore your fantasies. They are often the path to more variety and a more expansive dimension of sexual activity.

Red Hot LoveNote. . . *For Men Only* ~ It is time you realize the magic of those spontaneous moments, like blowing her a kiss from across the room or taking her hand, kissing it and telling how much you love her. Although they have no sexual overtones, she will feel the tenderness of the moment. Perhaps she will remember it when you are making love by whispering how special it made her feel. She may even allow it to inspire her. You will feel appreciated and, in time, your thankfulness for being appreciated will show up in more reciprocal tenderness from her. Become intentionally spontaneous. Make time for the feeling to strike you. Think of ways you can make her feel special. Never take for granted the lingering magic of those sudden impulses to recognize your lover for who she is.

Red Hot LoveNote. . . Making love must never be a silent experience. Say something. Make a joyful noise. Sound is an important part of communicating your feelings while making love. Speak up. Words help you to connect and break through your inhibitions.

Red Hot LoveNote. . . Fear takes away your choices to fully enjoy your sexual relationship together! The opposite of fear is love. Do everything within your power to ditch your fears and only love. Someone once said that fear is **F**alse **E**vidence **A**ppearing **R**eal. Love presents you with infinite possibilities. True love overcomes all fear. For a relationship to flourish, it must have trust. There cannot be total trust with fear present. Trust comes from having loving conversation together. It causes you to be free of the fear that saying whatever you feel the need to say will be taken the wrong way or that you will be rejected for it. Trust is the foundation of all healthy love relationships. There can be no trust without loving conversation; no genuine intimacy without trust.

Red Hot LoveNote. . . *For Women Only* ~ What can you do when he desires sex more often than you do? Will you forever be sexually out of sync? Not necessarily. Ask yourself how often you can make love "just for him" without becoming resentful or becoming uninterested. There are two kinds of orgasm for a man: one is for pure pleasure with his partner and the other is basically for stress release. A quickie is okay now and then, but many men would settle for a hand job. To a man, it is very erotic and sexually stimulating for his lover to give him an orgasm. Here are a few tips: Having lubricant handy is a must. A satisfying experience for a man involves the right amount of friction and pressure. Most men agree that harder is better. Nice and easy for you. Rough and tumble for him! When a man is ready to come, he wants to come. That is the reason for the rapid thrusting during the last few moments of intercourse. Feeling pressure to have sex can decrease intimacy. Masturbation is a healthy alternative to having sex with your partner when you really don't want to make love.

Red Hot LoveNote. . . Making love can be like a tonic to your relationship. Instead of the toxicities that with-holding your love and affection can bring, making love can liberate you from that awful state. Making love assists in the process of building trust. You feel much safer to relate with your lover on a higher level. When you "let go" of all of the stuff that keeps you from being close, it brightens your spirit; you feel more alive. Life is too short to be so short-sighted. When you communicate at the higher level of making love, you can feel free to discuss your mutual needs without fear that someone will step on your words. You actually begin to feel younger; you feel rejuvenated. It's like a breath of fresh air. You begin to grow *together* . . . not apart. Be assertive. Focus more care-fully on fulfilling the needs of your love partner, without giving up yourself, and *your* needs will have a much bet-ter chance of survival. Remember, we create our own real-ity. Make love. Not war! Celebrate your love for each other . . . tonight!

Red Hot LoveNote. . . Embarrassed to tell your lover what you really want? Communicate with the written word. Set aside an evening to be together to write each other a brief list of special pleasures you would like to experience while making love. Put on your most favorite music, light some candles, get in the mood. It is important to understand that the intention of this process is not to express complaints about what the other person is NOT doing right, but to suggest "something else" you could do together to make you both feel good. It will help you overcome your fear of saying what you want during sex. Begin by telling your lover several things he or she is already doing to bring you pleasure. Her list might read, "I love the way you kiss me. It tells me you care. I really enjoy being close to you and the way you run your fingers through my hair. An additional pleasure I would enjoy would be more time for foreplay. It helps me get ready. Touch me gently. Let me tell you when I am ready for you to enter me. I promise to give you a signal or say when next time. I love making love with you. Lead me to orgasm with only your fingers or a vibrator sometime. Very soon I want to let you watch me make love to myself. Very soon." His list might read, "I love to feel your fingernails on my back, pulling me closer, while you whisper, 'I love

continued

you so much.' I feel really special when you tell me you are horny, when YOU initiate sex. It's a real turn-on for me. An additional pleasure I would enjoy is for you to vary the pressure you use when you give me a hand job. I promise to tell you when to use more pressure and when I am about to come, to do it harder. I love knowing you are open for a quickie now and then. I want you to tell me when you are nearing orgasm. I really want to know. Sometimes I cannot tell. I want to please you and knowing I'm on the right track would help. I love the look on your face when you come." Write it down, then exchange papers and get up the courage to read your lover's list aloud. You may discover that you both desire similar things. "Oooh, great! I've been thinking about that one for a long time." You may also find something on the other person's list that you have wanted to do but were afraid to ask. "I didn't know if you would like that!" Love partners whose overall relationship is working well will hear their lover's words as inspiration. If your relationship is not working well, you may hear them as complaints. Sometimes it is easier to write each other a note than to say what you want. You have to crawl before you can walk. This process can help you let go of your inhibitions.

Red Hot LoveNote. . . Relationship problems always find their way into the bedroom. Being too busy in your life often expresses as exhaustion; petty situations as resentment; unresolved conflict as anger, all resulting in a declining desire and far less than the energy required for healthy sex. You may be together, but emotionally you are really not there for each other; both lying there, silently resigned to doing nothing to make it better, wallowing in your bitterness and resentment. It is not possible to solve a problem that you cannot both acknowledge. Can you imagine how your love life would be different if you would only talk about what's really going on? You don't know what you are missing! When you can learn to communicate about anything and everything at anytime, you can then not only share your love, you will find the full expression of the love you have for each other even more exciting. If you can't talk about it, you can't fix it! Great sex is about effective communications.

Red Hot LoveNote. . . *For Men Only* ~ Learn to use your mouth for sucking, tugging, stroking, licking, nibbling, embracing, fondling, gently gnawing, caressing, as well as kissing. Touch her with your mouth. Slow down. There is no fire to go to. You are already there. You are creating the flame. Give her one of those deep, wet kisses where tongues flicker and hearts beat wildly and time stands still. Women love an abundance of kissing before, during and after lovemaking, when bodies are toe to toe, knee to knee, chest to chest, fingertips to fingertips, nose to nose and even head to toe. It helps to make the sexual experience complete. Hang out at her bikini line for awhile, then move south for further exploration. Stir the ashes with your tongue. Steamy, smoldering passion lives there. Be discriminating. Use other parts of your body to give pleasure, too . . . not just your penis. She is destined to become an angel on fire!

Red Hot LoveNote. . . There is sex after 50, after 65, and beyond. You are never too old to make love unless you think you are. Relationships develop like fine wine. Couples grow closer and their partnership improves over time. The sexual intimacy that older men and women share may surprise you. Many healthy men and women remain interested in sex and sexually active well into their 60s, 70s and beyond. Making love with someone you have shared your life with for many years can continue to be a shared pleasure, even more so than when you were younger. Making love is not only about physical inter-course; it is about being close, hugging, kissing, fondling and touching. Orgasm for seniors is not out of the ques-tion. Although sex may not be as high on the list as it was in their youth, nor will they experience those raging bod-ily responses of earlier years, the happiest seniors seem to be those who remain sexually active. They are most likely to be the ones who exercise regularly and pay spe-cial attention to maintaining a healthy diet and getting ade-quate rest. As you grow older, you become less concerned about pleasing yourself and more aware of your love part-ner's needs. The love and commitment to continue to sat-isfy each other grows with the passage of time. Never let age be your cage!

Red Hot LoveNote. . . Hot tubbing is a great place to begin an evening dedicated to making love. It is a place for romance, relaxation, amorous massage, and together-ness. Turn up your favorite romantic music and begin with a chilled glass of wine and some warm conversation. The cool of the evening and the lustful touch of your lover's naked body in the heated water can lead to some mighty steamy sex. It is a place for experiencing greater sensu-ality. A water jet in just the right place is often enough to cause an orgasm for her. Feel the air bubbles tickle the inside of your thighs. Take your time. Hang out together in the heat of the moment. Experience foreplay at its best. Most lovers experience difficulty making love underwater, so seize the opportunity for other imaginative ways to plea-sure your partner. Say yes to unleashing his or her smol-dering (or should that be bubbling?) passion. Be ready for a time of extraordinary sexual expression on the edge of the tub or adjourn to the bedroom for the finale.

Red Hot LoveNote. . . *For Men Only* ~ When you have a problem, not communicating with your partner about it sends a message of its own. She then gets to make up what she thinks the non-spoken messages convey. Women are skilled in this activity. She might conclude that you do not love her as much as you used to. She might decide you just do not care anymore. HER lesson is to understand that when you *do* talk, it is time to honor YOUR feelings and just listen. On the other hand – what is she supposed to think? You won't talk! You often totally close down at the most inopportune times, sometimes because you don't know what to say or how to say it. Maybe you are afraid you might appear weak, or she might lose respect for you, and on and on. Maybe it is because every time you *do* allow yourself to become vulnerable enough to talk, she butts in with HER feelings! The typical woman has a need to

continued

verbalize, communicate, declare, express, vent, chatter, discuss, dialogue and debate the problem; she needs to continue to talk about it until *she* is finished talking about it. To her, this means she cares. It is the way SHE solves problems. YOUR lesson is to know that this is the way she is. Request that she only listen and hear you out. Let her know you will be willing to listen to how SHE feels at another time. Speak up. Do the thing you fear to do and the death of fear is certain. What you can talk about heals; it no longer holds you prisoner. Being emotionally honest and having intimate conversations can cause you to feel vulnerable. Show her you really care . . . talk to her. Be a real man, a man who communicates with his lover. In every scenario there are at least two lessons – one for her and one for you.

Red Hot LoveNote. . . Just because men are from Mars and women are from Venus does not mean that differences cannot be reconciled in the bedroom. It has been estimated that more than 50% of men think about sex daily compared to just under 20% for women. However, while there are differences, there are similarities. Making love is the highest expression of love for our love partner and is almost equally desired by men and women when the overall relationship is working. Our differences give us cause to celebrate our love and sexuality in individual ways. Doing the little things that will send our lover's heart into orbit makes love work. Working on the overall relationship together can help us to better understand the differences and will help us all feel more like making love. If we want more sex, we must learn to understand the differences and pay attention to the little things!

Red Hot LoveNote. . . Take care not to withhold how you feel about the sexual side of your relationship. It may be fearful in the beginning; however, the reward for not withholding how you feel gives you the courage to boldly express yourself again and again and again. If your love-making needs more spice, say so. If it needs to be more often or less often, say so. Everyone does not desire sex with the same frequency. You can negotiate frequency. To have something to negotiate, you must speak your needs. Withholding what is in your heart cheats you of the love and respect you deserve. Speak your feelings and needs freely. It helps you overcome the fear of being vulnerable. It is courage that gives you the freedom to tell your lover what you feel and what you need. You have to find courage. It doesn't find you. Fear is always between courage and you. When you love yourself enough that you can freely express how you feel in loving ways, courage shows up. Share yourself and your feelings with your partner courageously.

Red Hot LoveNote. . . *For Women Only* ~ Call your lover at his office and tell him to be prepared for a surprise when he gets home. When he arrives . . . you be the surprise! Put a note on the door he will enter: "Welcome Home! I have something special for you, something you love! Follow the trail!" Drop bits of clothing on the floor. Make it a sexy trail. Have the clothing lead to that special place where you can relax and make love. Tape a provocative invitation to your bedroom door so he can anticipate what is behind it. Be there waiting, dressed in something seductive. Draperies closed and candles lit; music playing. Two glasses of his favorite wine on the nightstand. Then quickly help him get undressed. Make passionate love together.

Red Hot LoveNote. . . Making love helps keep you healthy! Engaging in your favorite indoor activity not only measurably improves your physical well-being, it also confers equally meaningful emotional benefits. An increasing number of studies suggest that sexual activity may decrease the use of the excuse, "Not tonight, dear. I have a headache." The person with a headache rebuffs a partner's most tentative advances fearful that sex will further escalate their discomfort. However, in a study conducted at the Southern Illinois School of Medicine, out of 52 female migraine sufferers who made love during a headache, 8 women reported a total absence of pain and 16 experienced relief. Sexual activity had lessened the distress of nearly half the women. Sexual intimacy can be a sure route to feeling and looking better. Sex is a great stress releaser and reliever. Instead of popping aspirins . . . next time you have a headache, you might be better advised to seek relaxation in the arms of your love partner. Sex does a mind and body good.

Red Hot LoveNote. . . Do what you do with enthusiasm.
Everything. In all ways. Show interest in what you do
when you make love. You simply cannot put all of your
energy into the moment when you are thinking about
something else. Focus. Be in the present. Experience the
moment together. Plan your sexual menu. Take care to
have all the ingredients of great sex in place: love toys,
lubricants, oils, something cool to drink, anything that will
encourage intimate indulgence. Keep erotic discovery an
important part of your lovemaking. It will help you design
a healthy relationship with pleasure in mind. Experiment.
The exposure to one's vulnerability is intrinsic to the
process of becoming close. Enthusiastically light the fire.
Enthusiasm is catching.

Red Hot LoveNote. . . *For Men Only* ~ Put all of her five senses to work. Give her a warm oil massage while she is blindfolded and while you're wearing sexy silk boxers. She will smell the scented candles you have placed all over the room, listen to the soft, romantic music you have in the background and feel the gentle touch of your magic fingers and slow hands all over her body. Pause often to quench her thirst with her favorite cool beverage. Have your special massage be no less than an hour of foreplay. Keep an eye on the clock if you must, but make it last. Don't rush. Make love while she is still wearing the blindfold. Help her feel like the sexiest woman on earth when she is in your embrace. Be gentle, caring, selfless, and with beautiful words, whisper enticing ideas of love. Allow your partner to get lost in your lovemaking. Let her hear the sounds of your own pleasure and feel the good vibrations. Savor the erotic fragrance of your lover's scent. Be deliberate. Make her body feel like it is enveloped in a sensual trance and only you can pull her out. She'll be like putty in your hands!

Red Hot LoveNote. . . What comes first? Cleaning the dishes or making love? Sex plays an important role in any relationship. It is often important to leave the dishes sitting in the sink, to postpone mowing the lawn, to put aside the things you think "must be done," in favor of making love. It is this sudden surrender to the moment – and each other – that makes it a most important step to shared intimacy. Learn to be sexually affectionate spontaneously. Being responsive to the occasion is a mutual turn-on. Often those moments of unplanned ecstasy are some of the most memorable.

Red Hot LoveNote. . . Affectionate touch is a very important part of making love. You can touch with your fingers, a feather, your mouth, your palms, body to body . . . use your imagination! You cannot make love without it, so make the most of touch to enhance your partner's experience and your own. Never be afraid to touch yourself while making love with your partner. Most lovers would delight to know that not only their touch was contributing to your arousal, but also that you were so turned on you were touching yourself in places your lover had yet to discover. Touching yourself can often relieve your lover's fear of "not doing it right" or "touching you too hard or too soft." Let your fingers dance over your skin. Take your lover's hand. Show your partner which places give you the most pleasure to touch. Be the teacher.

Red Hot LoveNote. . . *For Men Only* ~ Often a woman's number one complaint is that her partner will not listen without a counterattack, claiming his innocence or defending his position. Listen to your lover. Never only just hear what she is saying. Do not talk. Truly listen. Listening is an art. It has been described as the capacity to be fully present and attentive with a still mind and an open heart. Don't just sit there and nod your head in agreement and at the same time find yourself thinking, "Okay! Okay! That's enough. Can't you see I am listening? Let's get this over with!" Practice only listening, not hearing and thinking simultaneously. That doesn't work. Be truly present with her. Learn to still your mind, to zero in on what your partner is really saying. Get rid of your interpretations and preconceived notions about what you think she is saying and what it all must mean. When you listen for what is really

continued

being said, miracles can occur. You hear and begin to understand. When it is your turn to say something, most likely you will speak with more wisdom and understanding. When someone knows you are really listening, what *you* say is more likely to be listened to and understood. Always be grateful that she is sharing herself with words from her heart, regardless of her tone (that's something she will need to work on). When your heart is open, and when you listen to your lover, you will hear the love she is expressing. Even when it's something that is painful to hear . . . be grateful. Be grateful that she has the courage to call attention to what is missing in the relationship. There are many love lessons to be learned. The more you listen with intention, the more quickly you will learn them. When she speaks, with a quiet mind . . . listen.

Red Hot LoveNote. . . Have a steamy affair with your love partner! Make love with reckless abandon . . . teasing, forbidden kisses, wild, oily, daring, hot, kinky, sensual, nasty, creamy, mysterious, tasty and fun! Not nasty in a way you would normally think of it, but in a sexy way. Not kinky in a way that offends your partner, but having sex in a new and exciting way, perhaps a little different than ever before. For example, if you have never used a vibrator while making love, that might be a little kinky to some. Not reckless, without thought of the consequences, but with total abandon, without fear and with a highly charged erotic awareness. The mind is the greatest aphrodisiac. Use your imagination to heat things up between you.

Red Hot LoveNote. . . Tell your honey you're horny! It feels great to be wanted, to know that your partner desires you. Making love is not about how horny you are; it's about how loving, warm and wonderful you are when you are horny. Make some noise. Honk if you're hot 'n' horny!

Red Hot LoveNote. . . *For Women Only* ~ Reaching orgasm can electrify you, enrapture and mesmerize you, set you on fire, downright turn you on and sometimes it eludes you completely. The pleasure of reaching orgasm is enjoying the trip more so than reaching the goal. It is most enjoyed if you can relax and enjoy the ride rather than try to live up to some expectation you may have about it. It is okay if you do not have an orgasm. For a woman, often foreplay is more enjoyable. You must make your love partner aware that it often takes you about four times as long to become fully aroused to the point of orgasm than he. Now that you both know this, it is best to focus on enjoying the sensations that come from the search for this erotic pleasure. What position might be best to help you reach climax? Many women find that being on top is more conducive to orgasm. You can move around more easily in ways that please you, which helps you to make contact with your lover's body the way you want. You can also control depth of penetration. When you are on top and facing him, your clitoral area is more accessible for manual stimulation. Many women find they need additional stimulation during intercourse to reach orgasm. If you have a concern about whether he does this or you . . . you are missing the point. Just enjoy the ride.

Red Hot LoveNote. . . How many calories can you burn off if you make love for ten minutes? The operative words are passionate and vigorous. Several estimates suggest that you can burn off about 45 and 60 calories for a 132-pound woman and a 176-pound man, respectively. Extend the time by another 10 minutes and you can almost double the calories. It is certainly more exciting than washing the family car, which burns off approximately the same amount of calories.

Red Hot LoveNote. . . If you want to get in touch with the body's potential for pleasure, lay on your healing hands of love. A slow, sensual massage is one of the best non-verbal forms of communication. Words are not necessary. The friction of a romantic massage needs plenty of oil and several towels to soak up any excess. You can focus on a full-body massage or specific parts. Your lover can enjoy the erotic pleasure of allowing only your fingers to dance over the skin or your partner can choose to let massage lead to orgasm. Begin with long, sensuous, circling motions on the back. Get in touch with your lover's body: shoulders, hands, hips, breasts, buttocks, feet and other important body parts. It is imperative to choose a time when you can both relax for a long time without interruption. It is an incredible alternative for expressing love and getting close physically with or without making love.

Red Hot LoveNote. . . *For Men Only* ~ Some men have been known to put off doing something their love partner has asked them to do, only to later do it and attempt to trade it for sex. That may work some of the time, but over the long haul it will not. Manipulation is a nasty game. That way of being isn't authentic. Your partner will recognize this evil deception and soon you will be back where you started. You must do things for her because you love her, never because you want something. If you have the slightest inclination toward great sex, try paying a lot more attention to the little things!

Red Hot LoveNote. . . To open our bodies to each other is to open our hearts to one another in a most vulnerable and intimate way. Learn to feel more than sexual pleasure. Exercise your ingenuity and feel the mysterious: the fulfilling richness of our hearts opening, touching, beating in harmony and expressing the passion, appreciation, desire, attraction and love we have for each other. The pathways to sensual ecstasy and bliss blend to create a fresh and fulfilling sexual experience. The power and beauty of this gathering of emotions fulfills not only sexual desire, but even our deepest yearnings for physical togetherness. To achieve this state of sexual awareness we must communicate with more love, give with more feeling and receive unselfishly. We accomplish this by exercising personal responsibility; an empowering context that leaves us with a say in the matter.

Red Hot LoveNote. . . To add a little adventure to your lovemaking, some daring couples like making love in the danger zone. Sexual escapades in semi-public places where the danger of being caught, watched or the potential of embarrassment adds excitement and intensity to sex. Becoming a member of the "mile-high club" (making love in the lavatory of an airplane), having sex on roofs and fire escapes, in darkened stairwells, on the deck of a yacht, at a religious retreat, in elevators, behind shrubbery in the park, on trains, in hospital beds, and in the parking lot of your favorite restaurant in broad daylight is risqué, risky and must be done fast, without interruption and without much foreplay. These amorous misdemeanors are both joyful, erotic, naughty, pulse-pounding and downright exciting. Having a quickie on the "edge" can both titillate and stimulate your sexual appetite for each other. Novelty and uncertainty are two components of eroticism. While there is always the risk of being discovered, this speedy walk on the wild side can add spice and excitement to your lovemaking. If you are capable of such wild and wacky escapades, please do so with care and at your own risk.

Red Hot LoveNote. . . *For Men Only* ~ You must develop an intuitive understanding of what women expect and desire when making love. Doing so is a prelude to great sex. If you want a completely stimulated partner, then you must do the stimulating! Be her dream lover. Explore her anatomy as you talk with her. Be sweet and gentle. Choose loving words. With those words encourage her to speak aloud when it feels especially good! Lovers generally make love to their partner the way they like to be made love to. Notice how she touches you, cuddles next to you, and when she lets you know with barely audible sounds that you are doing it right. For women, foreplay is an aphrodisiac; it fans the flames of sexual desire. Making love should be a total body experience. Having hot sex needs to be seasoned with reason. Use your head! . . . and your mouth . . . and your tongue. Take it nice and easy. Be creative in your love play. Take the plunge. Join the oral majority. Give her a delicious climax that will have her coming back for seconds.

Red Hot LoveNote... It is important to reach agreements about how and when you can fully express yourself in conversation about sex. Especially if there are unpleasant situations to discuss. One talks. One listens. Then, take turns. Do your best not to defend your position or get into any discussion about the pros and cons of what is being said. Give yourselves time to think about the conversation, then agree to get together again and make some new agreements and promises about workable solutions or new and exciting things to do. Avoid arguments. The rules of argument say that one must win and one must lose. Arguing will never assist you in reaching any reasonable conclusions. If something is not in your best interest or offends you, just say no. Never compromise your own integrity for the sake of anyone or anything.

Red Hot LoveNote. . . Deep within our hearts, all humans have a passion for love, companionship, and closeness. To feel the power of this desire is to increase the possibility that making love will become more than fulfilling raw sexual instincts; rather, it most assuredly will help you to consciously connect with the deeper feelings of love you have for one another. To first recognize this desire within yourself helps you to create a higher communion of love with your partner.

Red Hot LoveNote. . . *For Women Only* ~ Masturbatory orgasms tend to be more intense, with more distinct sensations of contraction and release than orgasms reached during intercourse. You may come more quickly than with your partner, taking as little as one fifth of the time. You know your body. You know precisely what to do to arouse yourself to reach this erotic state, how much pressure to apply and specifically where to apply it. When you reach solo orgasms you are more focused; you enjoy the sensations of the moment. The search for orgasm with your lover will be quite different. The process to climax may be prolonged by the presence of your lover in that now there are two people who are searching for the same pleasure. It can be distracting. This is why knowing what pleases you can is so important. Sharing your orgasmic secrets with your lover is a turn-on for him. Acknowledge this as an ingredient of foreplay. Let him know how important it is for you to be allowed to become fully aroused BEFORE he enters you. Exercise your right to slow things down. Make sure your partner knows that even though you may be willing to be the receptacle for his pleasure, he must reciprocate. Show him how. Demonstrate. There is no shame in not reaching orgasm during intercourse. However, the act of making love should be no less pleasurable for you if you do not.

Red Hot LoveNote. . . Constant bickering puts a hex on sex. Give up being stubborn. Cut your partner some slack! Would you rather be happy or right? Let go. Forgive. When you hang on to resentments or hold grudges against your love partner, it prohibits the free expression of sexual intimacy. It causes lovers to remain distant. Restoration following a disagreement takes time. Forgiveness speeds up the process. To restore your relationship to a state of love . . . let go of all that keeps your relationship stuck. If there is something standing in the way of your enjoyment of each other, set this book down right now, go to your partner and remove the hex! Forgive.

Red Hot LoveNote. . . Choose to have your bedroom be the "love zone," a play place. Use it only for sleeping and making love. A bean-bag in the corner of the room has some interesting possibilities; one that is big enough for two can be great fun. Look at your bedroom as a sanctuary of pleasure, seduction, passion, and desire. Create a quiet, relaxed atmosphere that will encourage sexual intimacy. Never contaminate the bedroom with heat generated by anger or resentment. Settle disagreements in a neutral place. Do not take your squabbles to bed with you. Honor this space reserved for resting, recuperating and making love.

Red Hot LoveNote. . . *For Men Only* ~ Your love partner must be the song in your heart. She must come before all else. She needs someone who will always be there for her. She deserves the best, most wholesome and healthy lover you can be. She wants you to take care of yourself. She needs the kind of lover she can count on to watch after her needs. If you want to receive what you need from her, (appreciation, acceptance and trust), then you must give her what she needs, (affection, understanding and most of all, RESPECT). These are only a few of our most primary needs. When the relationship is fine-tuned and on target, the sensual music you make together is the kind of music that inspires commitment, understanding, acceptance, forgiveness and love.

Red Hot LoveNote. . . There is rarely any danger of "sexual burn-out" as long as you make sure that you are expressing love, not just having sex, and placing emphasis on variety. In other words, you cannot do it too much and you must do it in different ways! Numerous studies have shown that the more regularly and frequently love partners engage in making love, the more likely they will be sexually active well into their senior years. Having lots of sex does not deplete you. The exact opposite is true. Many couples often say that making lots of love causes them to feel better and more energetic. The sense of well-being and vitality you achieve by engaging in active, recurring and unconstrained sexual closeness with your partner cannot be underestimated.

Red Hot LoveNote. . . Real lovers occupy not only a place in the bed they share, but in each other's hearts and minds as well. Constantly think of ways to surprise and excite your lover. While a marathon between the sheets is fun and exciting, the real challenge is to make love all day. You can do this by: noticing, then remembering to fill HER car with gas; thinking far enough in advance to order tickets to HIS favorite sporting event; warming the car for HER on a cold winter morning; preparing HIS favorite dish on a day other than his birthday; working together on an activity you know your partner does not particularly care for. Every amorous impulse can be a reminder to consciously connect with your partner not only with your attraction for each other, but with your appreciation, respect and desire for closeness. Make love all day by dreaming up new things to do and ways to surprise, titillate and excite your lover, ways that cause your mate to feel the love you are expressing by your unexpected actions.

Red Hot LoveNote. . . *For Men Only* ~ Foreplay begins with putting down the toilet seat. Being attentive to your love partner and her needs, regardless of what importance you may place on them, will also support things going well outside of the bedroom. Repeat . . . pay attention to the little things outside of the bedroom and whenever two creative minds choose to play together your sexual needs will be fulfilled. Your passion and your commitment to a love relationship capable of inspiring great sex can fuel your imagination and keep the fire of love burning. The reward? A gracefully feminine, benevolent angel given to the purpose of generously lavishing you with pleasure. Is it worth it? Think about it!

Red Hot LoveNote. . . Before sex comes foreplay. Following sex comes the afterglow – a time for endearments, a time for orally revealing your enjoyment of moments past, an opportunity for reaffirming your love. "Have I told you lately how important you are to me?" "I love making love with you!" Bask in the afterglow. Omitting this significant occasion of closeness can put a damper on future encounters.

Red Hot LoveNote. . . *For Women Only* ~ Not all women "love" performing fellatio; however, if you are one of those women, move past this roadblock to satisfying sex. Most women can become extremely competent at this sexual skill. If you are NOT one of those women, you must learn this most delicious way of pleasuring your partner. Men love to receive oral gratification and they strongly appreciate a woman who can bring them to intense orgasms in this way. Take a shower together, then make love to him using only your mouth, your tongue and your fingers. Begin by exploring his body with your hands as you passionately kiss him. Then, with your mouth, very slowly follow an irregular and purposeful path all over his body, until you reach the "right" spot. Some men do not like to have their breasts kissed. Ask. In time his penis will begin to be moistened by tiny drops of his oozing fluids. Don't stop. Have little concern for applying too much pressure with your hands while you apply gentle kisses to his penis. He'll let you know. Focus all of your energy on giving him the gift of the talents of your tongue. Many women find the scent of semen sexually stimulating. Not all women enjoy the taste of semen. Some savor it like a delicacy. There is nothing in an ejaculation that is in any way harmful to swallow. For men whose semen tastes sour, pineapple and other fruit juices taken regularly will sweeten the taste. The seminal odor that appears on your breath is quite sensual, erotic and can awaken and inspire your lover to further activity. Be sure you let him know how you feel about this. It is okay to ask him to let you know when he is ready to come. Real men honor their partner's request.

Red Hot LoveNote. . . Making love should be a joyful union of two uninhibited people in love, who feel free and passionately agreeable to accept, receive and share some of life's most breathtaking moments together. The quality of your relationship determines the quality of sex experienced together. You are not at the mercy of your thoughts. If you are constantly concerned with the stress of everyday living, it will reflect in your attitude about making love. Thoughts can be changed. It is your choice. You must make a conscious effort to turn yourself on with thoughts that arouse and stimulate you. It is called "getting yourself in the mood." Love partners who stay excited about each other deliberately stimulate themselves and their sex lives. When love partners take care of each other sexually, they both get their needs met; they strive for balance in their giving and receiving.

Red Hot LoveNote. . . *For Men Only* ~ Women want to feel close to their lover BEFORE they begin making love. This is number one! Talk to her. Hold her. Acknowledge her as a person. Women do not like to be suddenly thrown into bed only to have you roll over on top of her, grunt a few times, come and roll off again. Foreplay must begin before you get to the bedroom. She needs to be valued for her inner beauty. She needs sincerity. She needs to know that you respect her feelings and are not just after instant gratification. She longs for the attention you used to give her when you were first together. After you get to the bedroom, she wants and needs foreplay . . . lots of it; no less than 20 to 30 minutes of it! The secret to achieving mutual satisfaction is making sure SHE receives satisfaction first, before you begin making love, through whatever arousal patterns she needs – by stimulating the clitoris with fingers, oral sex or a vibrator. Few things can arouse a man and give him sexual confidence more than watching her come. Let her be your guide.

Red Hot LoveNote. . . You can love God *and* you can love sex. God created making love as a way of procreating and expressing your love and yourself with your forever love partner. There is no right or wrong way to make love other than what *you* think or say about it!

Red Hot LoveNote. . . *For Men Only* ~ A committed partnership succeeds only to the extent that a man can accept influence from his wife. Women are already very adept at accepting influence from their husbands. Men must learn that they are not the only one in the relationship with bright ideas. A successful relationship is not 50/50. It must be both partners committed to each contributing 100% to this sacred alliance and being willing to consider the views of the other. It is each giving to and receiving from the other; it is sharing and accepting suggestions, advice, support, and being influenced by one another in a healthy way for the good of the partnership. A successful marriage can only occur when a man is able to do this as well. Those who continue to hold on to being right about making all the choices or decisions and who refuse to negotiate concessions in the partnership will find happiness forever eluding them. A man's ability to be persuaded by his lover is critical to having a healthy love relationship.

Red Hot LoveNote. . . Some couples find it exciting to send not so subtle signals that say they are ready for sex. Like stepping out of the shower and exclaiming, "It sure feels good to be clean again! Wanna go play?" or "I am a clean machine! Wanna come up and see me sometime . . . like NOW?" Some are more subtle and less direct. Be brave. Say things that can let your lover know you are ready for fun and games. Be playful. Have fun inventing new ways of expressing your readiness for making love.

Red Hot LoveNote. . . *For Men Only* ~ Isn't it amazing the hours you spend on training for your life work compared to the time you spend on learning how to have a better and more successful relationship with your love partner? Consider being as energetic in the pursuit of a healthy relationship as you are in the pursuit of fame and fortune in the business world. Placing your business before your love partner causes her to feel neglected and resentful. Your overall relationship suffers as a result, to say nothing of how infrequent making love can become. She doesn't need your money. She needs YOU! Of course there is the responsibility of making sure your family has the appropriate financial support. However unless you place your lover in first place – over your business – you may not have to worry about supporting her or the family.

Red Hot LoveNote. . . Someone once said that women often fake orgasm because men fake foreplay! Couples who thrive in their experience of each other strive to seek the balance necessary for both to find mutual pleasure in their lovemaking. Both take full responsibility for getting what they want and giving what their partner needs.

Red Hot LoveNote. . . *For Women Only* ~ The percentages are getting higher. Statistics reveal that more women than ever are letting their fingers do the walking. Masturbation is often an embarrassing-to-admit and sensually pleasurable solo activity. To some, it is a sexual taboo. To the sexually liberated, it is a way to enhance sex with their partners because they self-stimulate, a sort of priming the pump. Some doctors suggest that it can increase your sexual appetite. Women who practice solo sex see themselves as entitled to sexual pleasure, which heightens their self-esteem. There is no wrong or right way to do it. Some women use a vibrator to stimulate the vagina while stroking or massaging the area surrounding the clitoris with their fingers with varying pressure. Circular motions, rubbing up and down one side or the other seem to be the preferred method. Finger motion generally becomes more intense until orgasm. Handheld pulsating shower heads with adjustable water pressure, water jets and the bubbles of hot tubs provide variety for genital stimulation. There is no medical evidence that self-gratification is bad for you. It is an excellent way to "know thyself."

Red Hot LoveNote. . . Be playful. Have fun with sex. When you get the urge to merge, take a tumble together on the living room floor. Be willing to risk getting a few rug burns. Make love on the edge of the tub in the bathroom on the spur of the moment. Playing strip poker, getting frisky and dancing naked on the back porch, being silly, and exploring other creative ways to enjoy your time together is what making love is all about. Uncover irresistible new ways to love each other between the sheets. Frolic together. Instigate some erotic tinkering with sex toys. Be amused with your own sexual curiosity. Utilize the seductive power of your imagination. Go to a sexy movie without undergarments, sit in the darkness of the last row and fondle, touch and caress. When you get home . . . go all the way! Marital sex requires infinite varieties of thought, commitment, adaptation and flexibility. Sex is a journey of intimacy you should enjoy in playful ways together!

Red Hot LoveNote. . . Same time, same place, same position? Yuck! Routine, predictability and passivity are at the core of boredom. Hot sex does not have to fade with time. Making love should be an enduring, delicious treat. Sexual expression is much more than *doing it!* It is a meaningful, deep communion where two people immerse themselves in the incredible sexual energy that only committed lovers can construct. This highly charged, emotional exchange causes a sensualistic awakening; an erotic resonance occurs between lovers. To alleviate boredom we must eliminate habitual, automated, commonplace, and monotonous sexual activity. Being vulnerable, unpredictable and spontaneous sows the seeds of desire and can breathe aliveness into the relationship.

Red Hot LoveNote. . . *For Men Only* ~ In a healthy love relationship, if you do not last very long during intercourse, it's not the end of the world, particularly if you were in slow motion during foreplay and made sure there was extensive attention to her needs. To many women, actual penetration is not nearly as intimate or satisfying as extended periods of foreplay. Most women feel slighted, hurt, frustrated or bitter when their lover only attends to his needs by being a two-minute wonder. Engaging in longer, more varied sexual sessions can lead to higher levels of arousal, deeper levels of intimacy and a stronger sexual relationship. Never stop exploring. Do not settle for the familiar. When it comes to incredible sex, emotional connection counts. That takes some time. Doing your best to make it last for her so sexual pleasure is extended is great. However, it can often backfire. Too long and you may miss YOUR moment; you hold back and delay too long and you wind up with a desensitized penis that quits before you are ready. When she is content, and you are coming down the home stretch and you accept the inevitability of ejaculation, it's okay to turn selfish for 10 to 17 seconds.

Red Hot LoveNote. . . *For Women Only* ~ One of the most sensual and sensitive places on a man's body is the perineum; that area between the scrotum and the anus. This area is loaded with nerve endings and is the closest thing there is to a male G-spot. Surprise your lover by massaging it or applying a vibrator while you are making love to him. It can be a source of intense erotic pleasure and increase the level of excitement especially during ejaculation.

Red Hot LoveNote. . . Always remember to give recognition, express gratitude and offer appreciation to your love mate for being who they are for you. Acknowledge them for the lover they are. A card or a brief heartfelt love note will do. Tell your lover something you especially enjoy about him or her. Tell her you love watching the way she moves while making love. Tell him you love the unexpected back rub with your favorite scented oil before you made love. Catch your partner doing something special and make a mental note to extend admiration in a handwritten remembrance at some unexpected time. Put some special thought into it. It is likely to become a keepsake, a talisman of passion. Loving words can reconnect two lovers when they come from the heart.

Red Hot LoveNote. . . *For Men Only* ~ Soften up your hands with a high quality hand lotion. Women love to be touched with soft hands. Make it a habit. Use it regularly. Be prepared. You never know when a warm and tender caress to the back of the neck might be just the thing that is needed to let her know you are behind her all the way and that you care. Slip up behind her and give her shoulders an old-fashioned, warm and tender rub. Do it longer than you think she expects you to. Go slow. Be gentle. Ask her to let you know where it feels good. Concentrate on how you think it must feel to have someone who really loves you rub your shoulders. A woman's body is like a temple. It must be respected. The last thing the most erotic areas of a woman's body need is to be roughed up with tough, scratchy hands.

Red Hot LoveNote. . . Plan some time for "making whoopee!" An appointment book for sex can change the way you look at making love. "That's ridiculous," you say. Not so. In this fast-paced world we live in, it seems that we often plan to do less important things and save making love for bedtime when most couples are worn out from the day's activities. Split shifts where she works days and he works nights can place a lot of distance between lovers. There's Little League, that last batch of laundry to be done and don't forget the late show where you crash and fall asleep before the end of the movie. Wrong! Excuses, excuses! Make time for making love. When you go out to eat, you make reservations. Why not make a date to meet in the bedroom at 8:30 p.m. on Friday night. How do you know you'll be in the mood? Anticipation helps, and you cannot be sure. But you don't know if you will be hungry when you make the restaurant reservation either! Never put your sex life on hold until you both FEEL like it. If you do, it will surely get lost in the daily grind. What about the children? Hire a family member or trusted friend who will babysit them overnight. Let your imagination soar. There is nothing wrong with scheduling some intimate playtime together. How about tonight?

Red Hot LoveNote. . . *For Women Only* ~ This may come as a surprise to you, but the odds are that your husband masturbates! Most adult men do. Married men are no exception. Why would he do this when he has you to make love with? Sometimes men (and women too) just want a quick and easy, uninhibited, uninvolved orgasm without their partner. This is not uncommon. Let's face it, orgasm is extremely pleasurable. Self-stimulation is a quick fix. Some men use girlie magazines or X-rated movies to help them get in the mood quickly. Usually this does not mean they have a sexual addiction. If you feel undesirable, neglected or excluded because of this, that, too, is not uncommon. You need only be concerned if he is consistently avoiding sex with you, or if he seems more attracted to masturbation than he is to you. This could be a warning sign that something is amiss in the relationship or that he has a more serious problem that needs to be mutually discussed.

Red Hot LoveNote. . . Intimacy flourishes when two lovers feel free to reveal their private thoughts with their partner, thoughts never intended to be shared with anyone else. Anytime you share a personal fantasy or sexual idea or activity with your partner, you are making yourself more vulnerable. Simply making love intensifies feelings of vulnerability. Women are very conscious of the way their body looks and men are sensitive to having their sexual skill criticized. Learn to leave your fears at the bedroom door. Be vulnerable. Respect your partner's courage to disclose ideas that might add spice to the relationship. Never, ever cause your partner to feel susceptible to attack or ridicule when he or she reveals a sexual fantasy or secret. It is okay to say no to something your partner may suggest when you feel the need to do so, but to oppress with disparaging words or belittle someone for disclosing their innermost thoughts will restrict future sexual revelations. Remember, there is a difference between thought and action. It is also okay to say yes to experience the previously unknown. The more you are willing to be open with your partner, the more responsive he or she will be to you. Vulnerability is the fast lane to intimacy.

Red Hot LoveNote. . . Halloween night can be a time for fun and frolic for two red hot lovers after the children have been put to bed. It can be very erotic to play "trick or treat" with your partner. Idea for him: Wear nothing but a brief mask and your tool belt, complete with all your sex tools (vibrator, lubricants, oils, etc.). Cover yourself with a robe (so the neighbors won't be shocked), sneak out the back door, walk around the house and ring the doorbell. When you hear the door opening quickly toss the robe aside! Have a tray, with two champagne glasses, a chilled bottle of champagne and her favorite flower. Say, "Trick or treat!" Won't she be surprised! Idea for her: Ask your lover to be prepared to go to bed a little earlier than usual. Tell him you have a surprise for him. After making sure the mood is right – sexy music is playing, lights off and candles lit, and he is comfortably situated in bed with a glass of his favorite beverage – adjourn to the bathroom. Paint some kitten whiskers on your face. Wear your most sexy, skimpiest nightie and a mask. Walk into the bedroom and say nothing except, "Meow!" Be his mysterious Halloween sex kitten. Proceed to make love TO him without any words . . . only an occasional "meow" or purring sound. Allow him to "turn a trick" and you get to be the treat.

Red Hot LoveNote. . . *For Men Only* ~ Many times the man wants to only make love and she wants to cuddle and to be romantic. Have agreements. Do it her way this time and next time do it your way. Or, for your relationship's sake, slow down and be romantic, cuddle, then make love. *Be patient.* Great sex should never be hurried. Sexual romance fully supports great sex. There is an art to giving a woman orgasm. It takes time. She must be fully aroused before she will be ready. Women only need to touch a man and he is ready. With her, take your time. Don't rush. Be romantic. Don't do it just to get what you want. She will know. Trust is important to this process. Trust is something you cannot give to someone else. It must be earned. She must love you and trust you enough to surrender to the moment. Attend to her needs. Slow down. Not too fast. It takes time to make love. Take time for her and she will make time for you. You unselfishly give . . . *then* you receive. It works best in that order. When you only jump on and get off, she most usually hasn't had time to get going. Intentionally delay your own pleasure for the good of the relationship and standby! Temporarily postpone your own gratification. Be second to experience orgasm. After the lovin' . . . cuddle. She wants to know she is loved and cherished. Negotiate for quickies at some other time. Remember to say those three magic words, "I love you."

Red Hot LoveNote. . . Do you seem to be sexually out of sync with your partner? With time, desires and needs do change. However, if sex was good at the beginning of your relationship, there is no reason why you both cannot work together to recapture the magic. To demonstrate your commitment to each other, plan to take a day off work. Pack a lunch and spend a day in the park. Find a vacant park bench or sit peacefully together under a tree and reacquaint each other with your true sexual selves. It will take some courage. Take a hand-in-hand walk. It is a step in the right direction toward reigniting the passion you once knew. Watch the squirrels gather nuts. Rekindle romance. Pick some wild flowers. Talk to each other about what you each enjoy when making love. Listen to the birds sing. This day together is an indulgence you cannot allow to pass. It is a way you can begin to rebuild a brand-new sexual relationship with your spouse. If you want to BE a couple, act like a couple. Rediscover each other. Design a plan to make sure your relationship never lacks passion and excitement. Focus your energy on getting sexually in touch again.

Red Hot LoveNote. . . *For Men Only* ~ Surprise your love partner with a full body massage! Use your fingers, hands and your naked, oily body to offer her some very special sensations. To prepare yourself for this erotic encounter, buy a book on the art of massage. Study it. Treat yourself to a massage, so you can get the feel of it. Remember how they use their fingers on the parts of your body where it feels good to you. Mix up your own special blend of oils. Try mixing about an ounce of Eleven Oils (made by Bergel of Hollywood, Inc.) with about 8 ounces of 100% Pure Expeller Pressed Almond Oil in a small, all-plastic bottle. It's not messy, absorbs into your skin, feels good and is great for your skin. Both are available at most health food stores.

Larry James

Warm it in your hands by applying a small amount to the palm of your hand and briskly rubbing your hands together. Learn the art of making love with your fingers. Touch her gently everywhere. Tease her. With practice, your hands can learn to listen to your lover's body and respond accordingly. Slow down where her body reveals it feels good. A soft, sensual full body massage can be foreplay, an incredible first step to making love. However, a slow, passionate full-body massage is not always a prelude to making love. Respect *her* wishes. Another variation of this idea is to treat her to a gift certificate to a professional massage therapist. Buy it in advance and present it to her when she has had an especially stressful day.

Red Hot LoveNote. . . Making love should be fun, frivolous and incredibly relaxing! Many people think that you have to have fabulous fireworks every time. This is not true. It cannot always be a wild, spontaneous event. Forget performance! That will only keep you stressed out! Performance anxiety is not a myth. Concentrating on super sex all the time will keep you from enjoying the comfort of being with the one you love. Instead, focus on having a great time with your love partner and making love will become more naturally sensual, playfully romantic and sexually satisfying. Lightening up under the covers can increase arousal and thrust making love to a higher level of intimacy.

Red Hot LoveNote. . . "But what about the children?" Hang a sign on the bedroom door that says, "We need some time together!" Spending time with your partner behind a closed door sends an important message to them. They need to know that you both place a high priority on being with each other. The sexual aura in the home of passionate love partners helps make open discussion of sex easier, more comfortable and credible. Your sexual desire for each other should not be a secret. When you openly express your love for each other, they feel safe. It gives them permission to form an intimate bond when they become young adults. For your children's sake, be passionate toward each other. When children grow up in an atmosphere of sexual intimacy, you are giving them the most precious gift that a parent can give. Every home is a school. What are you teaching your children?

Red Hot LoveNote. . . *For Women Only* ~ If you want to boost your husband's self-esteem as well as his sex drive . . . make the first move. Most men love it when their lover initiates sex. Seduce him. This is no time to be shy. Here are three sexy ideas. Begin flirting with him while he sips his coffee in the morning. Call him at the office. Tell him what you really want! He will be ready when he arrives home. So will you. Anticipation activates sexual energy. Wait until a commercial comes on, then, dressed only in your most sexy panties, walk into the living room where he is watching TV. Turn off the TV, kneel in front of him, put your hands between his legs and tell him you would like to have a quickie on the floor . . . right now! You have about 5 to 6 minutes of commercials before the show starts again. Most men won't last that long with a come-on like this. Long after the lights go out in the bedroom, begin by touching yourself and when you are ready, wake him up in the middle of the night gently stroking his penis. Seldom will he remain flaccid nor will he reject your advances. When you come on to him first, it helps him know that you want him as much as he wants you.

Red Hot LoveNote. . . *For Men Only* ~ Plan a surprise evening at home together. No TV. No phones. No kids. Have a trusted friend care for them overnight . . . at her house! The key here is to plan in advance. Have an agenda. No cooking. Cater in a bite to eat. Chill *her* favorite wine. Talk. Listen. Experience each other to the fullest. Make it an evening to remember. Do whatever you need to do to prepare an evening she will always treasure, one she will talk about for years to come. Making love is on the agenda, and it shouldn't feel as though you are squeezing it in hurriedly between the last TV show and the first sleepy yawn. Slow down. Take your time. Dim the lights. Scatter lit candles around the room. They can create an atmosphere of mystery of things to come. Burn some incense. Pick music that creates a passionate mood. Give her no less than thirty minutes of exquisite foreplay. Do what SHE likes. Pleasure her in erotic ways, orally and otherwise. This is not a night for you; it's for her. Try to imagine why you think "Love Me Tender" was such a big hit! Express your love by making warm and passionate love on the floor in front of the fireplace. Remember to light the fire. Have several blankets nearby in case you fall asleep.

Red Hot LoveNote. . . Enjoy each moment you are together for what it truly is. Share some of your lover's interests. What is it that your partner loves to do that you never do together? Make a special effort to help your partner plan that special something and do it together. Focus your mental energy on the thrill of just being together rather than the dread of doing something you would rather not do. Decide to have fun. It is your choice! You may be surprised to learn that when you do things with your partner only because you love him and want to be with him, you may discover another side of him. You may enjoy it too! The same is true for men. You may also find that your partner will be more receptive to doing some of the things that you would like to do. Some fishing trips really aren't about fishing at all. The same goes for shopping trips to the mall.

Red Hot LoveNote. . . The primary cause of a lack of sexual interest is unresolved problems in your relationship! Other causes include depression, anxiety, medications (especially for blood pressure, heart, anxiety, or depression), stress (overwork, mind on other problem(s)), low self-esteem (excessive weight gain, bad experiences from the past, fear), relationship problems (feeling unloved, resentment, anger), low testosterone (can be checked with blood test by your family doctor), fatigue (not enough sleep, "run down" – often used as an excuse!), and physical illness or debility (time to get a complete medical checkup). Another major cause is boredom with the same sexual routine. What can help? The answer: Regular exercise, proper nutrition (plus weight loss if appropriate), and

continued

good sleep habits, if it's not a medical problem. Place an emphasis on working on any problems you may be experiencing and you may be surprised. Stop withholding sex and things may change. If you are using sex as a weapon you will be sorry. What I am suggesting is that often a decrease in sexual desire is simply an excuse not to make love when the problems of the relationship appear too big to handle or you do not know what to do. When this is happening, neither party generally feels very good about making love. It is all about letting go! It takes courage and a commitment that is stronger than your weakest excuse about why you hold on to stuff that will only drag your relationships to the depths of despair. Give yourself a break! Let go OR get the assistance you need from your doctor or therapist.

Red Hot LoveNote. . . *For Men Only* ~ It is a mistake to come too soon. If you do, make sure you have a plan to contribute to her pleasure, too. Just saying you are sorry and fading into the distance is selfish and does nothing to extend sexual satisfaction to your partner. Making love is meant to be a shared pleasure. It is also a mistake to not come soon enough. Making love is not about performance; it is about mutual enjoyment. She may end up with a numb vagina and your penis may become so desensitized that orgasm may not be possible. It can happen. Reaching a happy medium somewhere between being a two-minute wonder and a marathon man is a wise choice.

Red Hot LoveNote. . . Sex is not a favor to be withheld. In marriage it is a sacred obligation. Granted, there are times when you may not want or feel like having sex with your partner. However, the love expressed by the sexual act is a needed supplement to sustain a healthy love relationship. Withholding sex, for whatever reason, can cause partners to withdraw from the relationship. If you feel that your partner is not making you feel special and appreciated outside of the bedroom, you may begin to keep score sexually to justify your resentment. It often can become a "she did" so when she is ready, "I will withhold too" and vice versa. This is a dangerous game for marriage partners to play. Making love exhibits your love for your mate. It helps that person know he or she is a needed part the partnership. With marriage there are fewer surprises than when you were flying solo. The longer you are together there is a preferential comfort to be mutually enjoyed, the warmth of shared passion and the grace of acting in accordance with what is just and moral and right and good for the marriage. It is important to the survival of the relationship to embrace and frequently experience sex. This expression of love and act of devotion to your partner will do more to keep you together than can any immature game you could make up to withhold the love that needs to be evidenced. If you do not keep sex active and exciting, the intimacy you feel from that special closeness will disappear . . . and quite possibly the relationship too.

Red Hot LoveNote. . . *For Men Only* ~ Kiss your lover slowly, sensually from head to toe. Body kissing can make her wet with anticipation. Sexual arousal will bring her genitals to life. Arousal is a prerequisite to great sex. Explore some ways for increasing sexual variety. Learn the art of the forbidden kiss. Slowly make the erotic journey to that sensuous treasure between her legs. Gently brush aside her genital hair and kiss away her stress. Give her the kind of lip service she will enjoy. This erotic stimulation will bring her heart and soul to life and drive her wild with desire. The more she can feel her desire for sex, the more fulfilling it is. The clitoral kiss is sexual magic in the making. To make it a tasty oral treat for you, try it with a menthol or cherry drop in your mouth. For many women, oral sex is a favorite form of sexual stimulation. A warm tongue bathing her clitoris, moving up and down, back and forth, wildly rotating, and flickering erotically to and fro can bring more pleasure than can fingers or your penis. It is a mistake to perform cunnilingus too gently once she is on fire. Next time she won't say, "No," she will say, "When?"

Red Hot LoveNote. . . Here are a few ideas that will titillate your lover's sensibilities! Move your love with motion. Prepare a bubble bath for her, offer to wash her back and towel her off. Tie a ribbon around yourself and give you as a gift. Play footsie under the table. Stay in bed all day. Meet him at the door naked. Try something you never have tried before. Have a playful pillow fight. Buy your lover a sex toy and attach a note describing how you would like it to be used. Kiss as though you have all the time in the world. Catch your lover doing something that pleases you and tell how it feels. Write naughty notes. Stop your car beside the road and pick her some wild flowers. Remember to speak, "I love you." Be his private dancer. If you want excitement in your marriage, you must remember to do the unexpected little things that mean so much to your partner.

Red Hot LoveNote. . . *For Women Only* ~ When the desire to have an orgasm is present, it is frustrating not to, not to mention the toll that not reaching climax takes on your psyche, sleep, complexion, sense of humor and everyone's ego (yours and his, unless you have an agreement not to or to take turns). Some women never have an orgasm. Doctors say about 30% do not. Some women can only achieve orgasm when they are alone. If you know how to brush your teeth, listen to the radio or wave "bye, bye," you may be in the 70% who can learn how to have an orgasm. There are several reasons you may want to try: to pleasure yourself when you prefer to experience solo sex without your partner and to discover how to reach orgasm so you can teach your lover to touch you in the ways you need to be touched so you can reach orgasm when together. Do you masturbate? Are you able to reach orgasm that way? If yes, you're halfway there. Slowly transfer your masturbation technique – what you do with your hands, your mind, your body – to lovemaking with him. Touch yourself while you're having intercourse rather than assume his penis alone will do the trick.

Red Hot LoveNote. . . Until you have the courage and the commitment to fully engage in your relationship, to be so intentional about it that it becomes the highest priority in your life, genuine intimacy cannot occur. Sexual intimacy of the highest order only occurs when the heat of passion melts the barriers around your hearts. With the freedom to pursue that special closeness only committed partners know, two hearts will meld together in a dance of Divine love.

Red Hot LoveNote. . . *For Men Only* ~ You may see her across the breakfast table every morning, and there are some things that you just cannot say over a bowl of oatmeal! This may be reason enough for you to write your partner an occasional love letter. You may feel more comfortable putting your amorous reflections onto paper. Sharing your innermost thoughts of love will often surprise her in a most delightful way. Do not hold back. Say it like you feel it. If you need some help, access a thesaurus and choose some new words to help you express your love. Loving words can create intimate connections with your partner. Those unexpected, tantalizing missiles of amour can keep your marriage flourishing and gloriously alive.

Red Hot LoveNote. . . Here's a note about personal hygiene. If your lover is sensitive to your feelings, you will most likely never hear, "It's not your technique, dear, it's your breath!" They may just choose not to make love with you anymore. Bad breath and body odors can keep your love partner from being able to fully enjoy physical intimacy with you. Talk about turnoffs! Foreplay is probably not the best time to ask, "Honey, did you brush and floss your teeth?" It may be difficult to relax enough to enjoy yourself with your partner while you are holding your nose! If you take sex with your partner seriously, take time to prepare for making love. Brush your teeth. Gargle some tasty mouthwash. Take a shower or warm bath. Apply a dash of cologne or perfume. Light some candles. To not make yourself ready for the highest level of the expression of love is showing gross disrespect for your lover.

Red Hot LoveNote. . . Never be guilty of only giving the sexual side of your relationship your leftover energy. Unless you make your sexual relationship a priority, it will lose its spark. Sex is important and necessary for a relationship to prosper. Most partners hunger for sexual intimacy. Making love brings you together. It is the giving and the gift. It opens our hearts and our minds. Sex can be beautiful when love partners put some effort, enthusiasm and energy into the process. Anticipation is a powerful aphrodisiac; it is a turn-on. It generates sexual energy. Give yourself something to look forward to. Plan to make love. Spend some time thinking about it. If you must, make an appointment. And when you do get together, put all your energy into making it a combustible coupling, one you will cherish forever.

Red Hot LoveNote. . . *For Men Only* ~ Married men often do not take time to seduce their partner. The act of gentle seduction causes her to feel sexually desirable, wanted, cherished and demonstrates genuine respect and affection. Feeling this way turns a woman on. Take time to become deeply interested in her feelings. Spend time with her. When you do, every sexual aspect of your relationship becomes the normal course of action. Put some excitement and thoughtfulness in setting the stage to become united. It can begin with a love note, an unexpected greeting card or a sexy phone call suggesting intimacy the day before. Read a book on seduction. Pay attention to the techniques of some of our greatest lovers. It was Ricardo Montalban who said that a great lover is someone who can satisfy one woman her entire life and be satisfied with one woman his entire life. It takes imagination, creative seduction and sensitivity to her every sexual need. The subtle action of seduction enhances lovemaking and promises more sexual satisfaction for both love partners. Together you will cherish those private moments only committed partners can treasure.

Red Hot LoveNote. . . One of the secrets that makes oral sex great is knowing that your lover is deriving as much pleasure from performing it as you are receiving it. The secret is the enthusiasm they exhibit while doing it. Arousal is heightened. It is sexually stimulating to know that they love giving you pleasure. You want to know that they are also enjoying themselves and not just doing you a favor!

Red Hot LoveNote. . . *For Men Only* ~ Have you become only a part-time lover and a full-time couch potato? Is channel-surfing becoming more important than your relationship? This is a very bad sign. Everyone deserves to crash once in a while, but if you are habitually plopping in front of the TV when you get home, letting HER cook supper, clean the dishes and put the kids to bed, you are putting your relationship in the danger zone! She may become resentful, and eventually sex will go out the window! The remote control can be a relationship wrecker. This is a habit you must break. If you want more love, and more sex, at least once each week, surrender this little time-waster to your beloved. Tell her to hide it from you and while she has it, be willing to do whatever SHE would like you to do that evening. She may be amazed at your willingness to give up temporary control of your life, but it will be worth it. Help her with dinner. Clean the kitchen. Do the dishes. Listen to her tell about her day; don't just bitch about yours. Talk. Take a walk. Sit leisurely on the back patio and listen to the wind, but be with HER. Enjoy some time together. Do not expect sex just because you are releasing the remote to her. Expect nothing and see what happens! Living with a remote control hog is a lonely life. Ask HER. She knows!

Red Hot LoveNote. . . . It is not okay to only have "quick-ies." Having an occasional quickie demonstrates a healthy attitude about sex. But only having quickies does not let you off the hook if you are prone to always be too busy to have a romantic sexual interlude that lasts beyond two minutes! Use common sense. If you only always have quickies, that's just having sex. A loving, healthy rela-tionship demands balance. Making love . . . really mak-ing love, taking time for each other, provides the appro-priate balance needed to have a relationship thrive.

Red Hot LoveNote. . . After your partner's shower, invite him or her to relax in their favorite chair. Tune the headphones to your lover's favorite music. Warm some scented oil and give your partner's feet a massage they will never forget. Get to know this special part of their body. Apply gentle pressure between and underneath the toes. Using your thumb on the heel of the foot, push gently against the skin, holding it there for a few minutes, then slowly move it to another part of the foot. Repeat this process until you have covered the entire foot. Set a goal of about fifteen to twenty minutes per foot. When you think your lover thinks you are about ready to quit, continue to tenderly massage for an another five minutes or so. Let love flow through the tips of your fingers. There are many pressure points on the bottom of the foot that can assist in relieving the stress and tension of the day.

Red Hot LoveNote. . . *For Women Only* ~ To let your partner know you are ready for love, do some heavy flirting with your eyes. Wink. Give him that come hither look. Motion with your finger. Blow him a kiss. Men are intoxicated by the enchanting look of love in their partner's eyes. He can tell you are ready for love. Lighten up! Be obviously available. Give him the green light with your baby blues. Be seductive. Slowly wet your lips. In the midst of flirting, toss your hair and drop a few intriguing hints of things to come. Smile. Get close enough to let him pick up the scent of his favorite perfume. Be a little mysterious. It demonstrates a quiet confidence that will make him know that there are many things about you that he has yet to learn. He will soon be under your spell. Learn to lure your lover with your eyes, gestures, quiet conversation and never be afraid to initiate an intimate sexual rendezvous.

Red Hot LoveNote... When you trust your love partner, you feel more open and much less inhibited. Trust is essential to having electrifying sex together. When you know your partner loves you and will not rush to judgment when you have a sudden burst of creativity and dare to attempt something out of the ordinary, you feel safe in experimenting with new ways to offer love. The trust and respect you have for your partner's daring can stimulate inspiration and can move your sex life from satisfying to sensational! Trust and respect are two secrets of great sex.

Red Hot LoveNote. . . Let love catch fire in the bedroom! The more sensually adventurous you become, the more you participate sexually, the more intense your sexual responsiveness becomes. The more great sex you have, the more great sex you will want. It takes a willing partner, mutual trust and sufficient motivation to learn new attitudes and approaches to making love work. Making love is a skill to be learned, a pleasure to be mutually enjoyed. Playfully practice. Lighten up. Relax your body and your mind. Stress can decrease your sexual responsiveness. Let go of your repressed sexual feelings. Sex is not shameful and dirty! Reinvigorate your relationship. Generate a lot of heat together!

Red Hot LoveNote. . . *For Men Only* ~ Most likely your partner does not expect to reach orgasm every time you make love with her. Ask her. This is one more reason fore-play is important. She knows that sex can still feel good, she can benefit from the pleasure of the encounter and can feel complete without reaching climax. This drives some men wacky. What you may perceive as a lack of sexual interest is seldom anything to be concerned about unless it becomes a habitual occurrence. A preoccupation with giving your wife an orgasm may bring on feelings of inad-equacy. The operative word is "preoccupied." She will need to let you know when she wants orgasm and when she is willing to settle for touching, stroking, and caress-ing while you make love with her and have an orgasm of your own.

Red Hot LoveNote. . . Anti-masturbation activists would have you believe that self-gratification is wrong. Masturbation is making love with someone you love. It is exploring your own sexuality. Most everyone does it. Few talk openly about it. Single-handed sexual gratification injures no one, not even the practitioner. Self-masturbation is a concert with one-part harmony. Know your instrument. Learn to play it well. The melody becomes even sweeter when there is two-part harmony played in recital with your lover. Erotic, self-stimulation to orgasm is clearly a built-in component of human sexuality. Reaching climax in this way is one of the highest forms of self-pleasure. Let's put away the old-fashioned idea that masturbation is not good for you. Of course, anything to an excess is bad. To masturbate in lieu of making love with your partner is wrong; however, when used for self-enjoyment on an occasional basis or in concert with your partner, it offers a healthy release. People seem to masturbate more when they're getting good sex, because they are more aware of their bodies and because their brain chemistry is geared to the pleasure it gives.

Red Hot LoveNote. . . *For Men Only* ~ When your love partner is at the height of sexual arousal, it might be fun for both of you to initiate an expedition to locate her G-spot. It is located inside the vagina on the upper wall (toward the navel) about a half inch to an inch from the opening. When stimulated, the G-spot swells to about the size of a half dollar and has the puffy consistency of a marshmallow. To find it, insert a finger and curl it toward you. This area responds best to firm pressure. It is best to make sure your partner is wet and very ready before you go exploring. When this area is stimulated with your fingers or a G-spot vibrator (some are specifically shaped for this purpose), most women may feel the need to urinate. This sensation only lasts for a few seconds. Unless she knows this is a normal sensation, she may instinctively steer you away from the area before you can stroke it long enough to bring a response. At least you know you have discovered the right spot. Have fun!

Red Hot LoveNote. . . *For Women Only* ~ Sex, especially great sex, begins in the brain. To achieve sexual fulfillment in your relationship, you must maintain a healthy, positive attitude about making love. Your sexual pleasure is not a gift that your lover gives you. You must recognize your own body's tremendous capacity for sexual pleasure and give yourself permission to enjoy it. When you understand your own sexuality fully and know that your pleasure is not the responsibility of your partner, you can begin to fully recognize the conditions under which you can let go; to be in touch with the ways you need to be stimulated for arousal and orgasm to occur. Allow yourself to be sexual. Embrace all the sexual knowledge you can and learn to be at ease with your sexuality. Have great confidence in your sexual choices, the ways you communicate in non-threatening ways from your marriage bed what you need. Being a sexually satisfied woman calls for sharing your sexual needs with your partner and being willing to experiment with him in ways that satisfy both of you.

Larry James

Red Hot LoveNote. . . You can survive without sex, but why would you want to? Making love with your partner not only feels good, it is good for you. Be an active participant in your own enjoyment. Share yourself fully with your lover. Responsiveness is heightened when couples recall the magic that drew them to each other in the beginning. Continue to share tenderness, warmth, admiration, emotional attention, closeness, playfulness, sensual touch and humor. Never stop! Memories become the aphrodisiac that can help you to maintain desire, sexual interest and vitality in your relationship.

Red Hot LoveNote. . . *For Men Only* ~ Here's a hot tip! Making your sweetheart the center of attention when you arrive home from the office, regardless of what kind of day you have had, can work wonders for your relationship. Go to her first! The children will have to wait their turn. Give her a kiss of greeting. It reconnects you physically and mentally. We are not talking about a little peck on check to say hello before proceeding to the living room to crash in front of the TV. Give her a deep, wet, lipstick-smearing, outrageously sexy kiss! Embrace her. Whisper those three magic words, "I love you!" It could become your healthiest sex habit.

Red Hot LoveNote. . . Take the time to make yourself desirable. Never let yourself go. In some long-term marriages, couples will often go to bed without showering or bathing, with face or legs covered with stubble, with unbrushed teeth and offensive body odor. No wonder you're not getting any! Showing little consideration for your partner in this manner is sure to put the skids on the sexual side of your relationship. Not having enough respect for yourself to regulate weight gain is another form of taking the relationship and your partner for granted. It is possible to feel desire, but to not present yourself as desirable and yet expect to receive sexual favors is wrong. Perhaps a little more sexual etiquette is in order.

Red Hot LoveNote. . . *For Men Only* ~ If you are prone to ejaculate prematurely, you must participate in lots of foreplay with your lover before you have intercourse. Premature ejaculation often occurs when you do not take into consideration the feelings of your partner. Because sex feels so good, you keep going and going and going (like the famous Energizer bunny) and soon reach climax without any consideration as to whether your wife is having fun, too. This is not a healthy idea. It can only be prevented when you can allow yourself to be last and the pleasure of your partner to come first! You CAN do something about this. You must allow her to be completely satisfied before you have intercourse with her. Then, when she is a happy camper . . . you get to be next! You need to remember that your orgasm is the bonus for making her feel relieved, relaxed and fully satisfied. You can have your orgasm only AFTER she has had her orgasm or has had enough foreplay and signals you to enter her. It takes most women anywhere from 20 to 30 minutes to become wet and fully aroused, so take your time. If you both have a desire to make intercourse last longer, when you feel like you are going to come, stop, then begin again. Remember, you are making love with someone special, not just having sex, and SHE is entitled to have some fun, too. This isn't just for you! If you do not get a hold on this problem (pun intended), she will most likely become resentful and angry and your relationship will begin to go down the tubes. Lazy lovers come, roll over and go to sleep without making sure their partner is satisfied. Do not have intercourse until SHE says to enter you. When that occurs, go for it. To do so before is showing gross disrespect for your partner's sexual feelings.

Red Hot LoveNote. . . Making love is the highest level and the most loving way we can physically communicate our love for our love partner. It is the ultimate expression of togetherness! The sexual experience can be the single most exciting, most powerful, most exhilarating, most renewing, most energizing, most creative, most affirming, most intimate, most uniting, most stress-relieving, most affectionate, most romantic, most recreative physical experience of which humans are capable. If you truly have a need to be in touch with these feelings, then it is imperative that committed couples do "whatever it takes" to make their overall relationship work.

Red Hot LoveNote. . . *For Women Only* ~ Men are very visual. They get fired up very quickly by visual stimulation. If you want to get your man red hot, lead him to bed, pour him a cool glass of his favorite wine and allow him the pleasure of watching you undress. Dim the lights. If you need help with a button or zipper, ask. Most men find this seductive exhibitionism particularly erotic to watch. Sexy is in the eye of the beholder. Movement attracts attention. Let him see you brush your hair. Flirt. Place a piece of jewelry on the nightstand, lightly stroke your thighs as you walk, and when you are close enough, kiss your fingers and place them on his lips. Smile with your eyes. Smooth lotion over your skin and teasingly spray perfume on parts of your body you know he loves to be near. Consciously arouse him with the way you tantalize your body with your own gentle touch. Let him see your eyes close as you softly touch your nipples beneath your see-through satin top. Tease him. Your private bedtime ritual can be a very seductive overture of pleasures to come. One way to keep him deliriously happy in bed is to invite him to be a midnight voyeur.

Red Hot LoveNote. . . Need help in tracking down a sex therapist? Ask your doctor for a recommendation, or for a free listing of AASECT certified sex counselors or sex therapists in your state, send a self-addressed, stamped business-sized envelope to the American Association of Sex Educators, Counselors and Therapists, P.O. Box 238, Mount Vernon, IA 52314-0238. When selecting a therapist, it is wise to decide whether you will feel more comfortable talking to a man or a woman. Most importantly, do your personalities click? Is this someone you will feel comfortable confiding in? Are you willing to truthfully answer ALL questions asked so the therapist can better assist you? Will you follow the suggestions given by your therapist? Would you feel comfortable going as a couple or individually, or a little of both? If you need help, please ask for it.

Red Hot LoveNote from the Author's Heart. . . What does it take to have a healthy sexual relationship? It takes a relationship with unwavering commitment, a passion for life's sexual journey and a dedication to the processes to go from boring sex to bliss in the bedroom. It requires dedication to pleasure; learning to be intentionally spontaneous; developing the ability to communicate openly and honestly your most secret sexual desires; the willingness to be a student of great sex; the discipline to stay in the moment when being sexually intimate; the daring to experiment; an attention to hygiene; the generosity to consider your lover's pleasure before your own or the esprit de corps to decide whether you go first or reach orgasm together; the keenness of mind to recognize the value of making love vs. only having sex; the gusto to be energetic or the sensitivity to passionately lie motionless together; the wit to not always take yourselves so seriously, to laugh, to play and to experience whatever is sexually fun; the insight to negotiate agreements and promises about how you will mutually care for your partner's needs in the sexual arena; the courage to ask for the variety of pleasure you want and deserve and the respect to honor your lover's right to say no without consequence.

Recommended Reading, Listening and Viewing

Allen, Chris, **1001 Sex Secrets Every Man Should Know.** NY: Avon Books, 1992

Bechtel, Stefan & Stains, Lawrence Roy, **Sex: A Man's Guide.** PA: Rodale Press, 1996

Block, Ph.D., Joel D., **Secrets of Better Sex.** NY: Parker Publishing, 1996

Borys, Henery James, **The Sacred Fire.** NY: HarperCollins, 1994

Chartham, Robert, **The Sensuous Couple.** NY: Ballantine Books, 1971

Chia, Mantak & Arava, Douglas Abrams, **The Multi-Orgasmic Man.** CA: HarperSanFrancisco, 1997

Chichester, Brian & Robinson, Kenton, **Sex Secrets.** PA: Rodale Press, 1996

Comfort, Alex, M.B., Ph.D., **The Joy of Sex.** NY: Simon and Schuster, 1972

Comfort, Alex, M.B., Ph.D., **More Joy of Sex.** NY: Simon and Schuster, 1974

Corn, Laura, **101 Nights of Grrreat Sex.** CA: Park Avenue Publishers, Inc, 1995

Corn, Laura, **101 Grrreat Quickies.** OK: Park Avenue Publishers, Inc., 1996

Corn, Laura, **101 Nights of Grrreat Romance.** OK: Park Avenue Publishers, Inc., 1996

Corn, Laura, **237 Intimate Questions Every Woman Should Ask a Man.** OK: Park Avenue Publishers, Inc., 1996

Corn, Laura, **The "G" Spot** (Video). OK: Park Avenue Publishers, Inc., 1996

De Angelis, Barbara, Ph.D., **How to Make Love All the Time.** NY: Dell Publishing, 1987

De Angelis, Barbara, Ph.D., **Real Moments for Lovers.** NY: Delacorte Press, 1995

Godek, Gregory J.P., **Romantic Fantasies & Other Sexy Ways of Expressing your Love.** IL: Casablanca Press, 1997

Gray, John, Ph.D., **Mars and Venus in the Bedroom.** NY: HarperCollins, 1995

Gray, John, Ph.D., **Secrets of Successful Relationships** (Audio Cassettes). CA: Heart Publishing.

James, Larry, **How to Really Love the One You're With.** AZ: Career Assurance Press, 1994

James, Larry, **LoveNotes for Lovers: Words That Make Music for Two Hearts Dancing.** AZ: Career Assurance Press, 1995

Kramer, Johnathan, Ph.D., & Dunaway, Phil & Diane, **Why Men Don't Get Enough Sex & Women Don't Get Enough Love.** NY: Pocket Books, 1990

Lloyd, Joan Elizabeth, **Come Play With Me.** NY: Warner Books, 1994

Lloyd, Joan Elizabeth, **If It Feels Good: Using the Five Senses to Enhance Your Lovemaking.** NY: Warner Books, 1993

Smith, Earl & Rose, **Sizzling Monogamy.** NM: William Havens Publishing, 1997

St. Claire, Olivia, **203 Ways to Drive a Man Wild in Bed.** NY: Harmony Books, 1993

Yaffe, Maurice, & Fenwick, Elizabeth, **Sexual Happiness for Women.** NY: Henry Holt and Company, 1992

"Bursts of truth, flashes of insight and words of wisdom for those on the path to wholesome and healthy love relationships. A thought-provoking, refreshing adventure in love and self-discovery. A must-read book for all!"

John Gray, Ph.D., Author
Men Are From Mars, Women Are From Venus

How to Really Love the One You're With: Affirmative Guidelines for a Healthy Love Relationship is a revealing and personally empowering look at self-liberating insights that will assist you in achieving a healthy love relationship anchored in unconditional love. Its wisdom will inspire you to deeper levels of self-acceptance and understanding. These words of love will benefit anyone, married or single, either couples already in a committed relationship or singles who may be in search of a healthy love relationship.

Larry James has transformed words of love into a message of hope that offers encouragement, inspiration and the opportunity for enlightenment in relationships. He presents a priceless treasury of inspiring and insightful thoughts, ideas, indispensable guidelines and reflections on how to really love the one you're with.

"LoveNotes for Lovers can move your relationships in the direction of acceptance, understanding, fulfillment and unconditional love."

John Gray, Ph.D., Author
Men Are From Mars, Women Are From Venus

LoveNotes for Lovers is a collection of meditations, affirmations and reflections on love. A valued relationship is something you work on all the time, not only when it's broken and needs to be fixed. *LoveNotes for Lovers* assists in that process. Every LoveNote is but one more piece of the relationship puzzle. The design of *LoveNotes for Lovers* is to help people fit the pieces of the relationship puzzle together in a healthy way. Each one is a mini-lesson in love.

LoveNotes for Lovers is a book for together lovers . . . husbands, wives and committed lovers – those who have found their true love . . . for love partners whose love has grown cold – those who would like to recapture the excitement that brought them together in the beginning . . . for lovers in waiting – those who are alone, no longer lonely and ready for a committed relationship.

In the tradition of his best-selling book, *How to Really Love the One You're With*, Larry James' *LoveNotes for Lovers* presents self-liberating insights, easy-to-read quotations, brief inspirational essays, and thought-provoking ideas.

Available in bookstores. For a copy personally autographed by the author, call 800 725-9225. Visa or MasterCard accepted.

LoveNotes for Lovers
(Paperback) $9.95
Career Assurance Press ~ ISBN 1-881558-03-7

About Larry James . . .

Larry James is founder and president of the Career Assurance Network. He is an author and professional speaker; a gifted teacher who shares his inspired insight with clarity, style and good taste. Larry James is a specialist in matters of the Heart.

He is on the staff of Dr. John Gray, Ph.D., author of *Men Are From Mars, Women Are From Venus*, and was Dr. Gray's personal choice to host the popular "Mars & Venus Chat Room" on America Online. Larry was personally trained by Dr. Gray to facilitate Mars & Venus Seminars.

Larry has appeared on more than 400 radio talk shows. His relationship articles have appeared in numerous magazines, newspapers and on the Internet.

Larry is a member of the National Speakers Association. He travels nationally leading seminars and giving speeches of inspiration that focus on developing close personal and business relationships. He champions the value of networking and has been called the "Guru of Networking."

Puzzled . . . about relationships??

Sometimes the pieces don't fit together so well . . .

sometimes they do!

PRESENTING

A Relationship Enrichment LoveShop™

A workshop designed to help you fit the pieces of the relationship puzzle together in a healthy way.™

Author and professional speaker Larry James presents his popular **Relationship Enrichment LoveShop** in major cities nationally. It is an interactive workshop with open discussion about how to achieve a healthy love relationship. Each LoveShop is a place where married couples, singles with partners or solo singles – who are committed to having excellence in their relationships – can freely and openly discuss the various pieces of the relationship puzzle. Larry reviews the five pieces of the relationships puzzle that are guaranteed to enhance your relationship when you put them to work.

The LoveShop is adapted from his best selling books, *How to Really Love the One You're With: Affirmative Guidelines for a Healthy Love Relationship, LoveNotes for Lovers: Words That Make Music for Two Hearts Dancing* and *Red Hot LoveNotes for Lovers.*

Larry also presents **Mars & Venus Seminars** based upon the work of Dr. John Gray, Ph.D., author of *Men Are From Mars, Women Are From Venus.* He is on staff with Dr. Gray and was personally trained by him.

If your organization, church, married or singles group would like to sponsor a **Relationship Enrichment LoveShop** or a **Mars & Venus Seminar,** call 800 725-9223 for complete information.

About Career Assurance Network . . .

Career Assurance Network is a company specializing in personal and professional relationship development seminars, workshops, keynote addresses and Mars & Venus Seminars.

Career Assurance Network, whose acronym is CAN, is committed to providing services and products that will assist you in being the best you CAN be! Larry's books and audio learning systems are available from the publishing arm of our network, Career Assurance Press.

About Larry James' Relationship Learning Systems . . .

A complete list of Larry's audio learning systems, books and other products is available upon request.

If you are interested in a list of available seminar or keynote topics or in contacting Larry to arrange a personal appearance, please write to the address below or call our toll-free number.

Larry James would love to hear from you!

If this book or any other works of the author have made a difference in your life or if you have ideas you would like to contribute, please take a moment and let him know. Send all correspondence to the address below.

Larry James
Career Assurance Network
P.O. Box 12695
Scottsdale, Arizona 85267-2695

602 998-9411 ~ 602 998-2173 Fax ~ 800 725-9223
E-Mail: CANetwork1@aol.com